READING THE
WAMPUM

*Essays on Hodinöhsö:ni' Visual Code
and Epistemological Recovery*

PENELOPE MYRTLE KELSEY

SYRACUSE UNIVERSITY PRESS

All royalties from the sale of this book will be donated to Neto Hatinawakwe
Onkwehowe Native Arts.

Material quoted from James Thomas Stevens's *Tokinish* (First Intensity Press, 1994)
and *A Bridge Dead in the Water* (Salt, 2007) reprinted with permission.

For a listing of books published and distributed by Syracuse University Press,
visit www.SyracuseUniversityPress.syr.edu.

ISBN: 978-0-8156-3366-2 (cloth)   978-0-8156-5299-1 (e-book)

Library of Congress Cataloging-in-Publication Data
Kelsey, Penelope Myrtle.
    Reading the wampum : essays on Hodinöhsö:ni' visual code and epistemological
recovery / Penelope Myrtle Kelsey. — First edition.
        pages cm. — (The Iroquois and their neighbors)
    Includes bibliographical references and index.
    ISBN 978-0-8156-3366-2 (cloth : alkaline paper) — ISBN 978-0-8156-5299-1 (ebook)
    1. American literature—Indian authors—History and criticism.   2. Indians in motion
pictures.   3. Iroquois art.   4. Iroquois Indians—Intellectual life.   5. Iroquois Indians—
Social life and customs.   6. Iroquois philosophy.   7. Wampum belts—New York (State)
8. Visual communication—New York (State)   9. Knowledge, Theory of.   10. Narration
(Rhetoric)   I. Title.
    PS153.I52K45 2014
    810.9'897—dc23
                                                                  2014025318

Manufactured in the United States of America

for Levi

Penelope Kelsey is associate professor of English at the University of Colorado at Boulder. She is of Seneca descent (patrilineal) with familial roots in western Pennsylvania and New York. She is the author of *Tribal Theory in Native American Literature* (University of Nebraska Press, 2008), and she edited the collection, *Maurice Kenny: Celebrations of a Mohawk Poet* (SUNY Press, 2011), which won the Wordcraft Circle of Native Writers and Storytellers Best Literary Criticism Award in 2012.

Contents

Illustrations

Introduction

Hodinöhsö:ni' Visual Code
and Intellectual Transmission

This book was born out of a deep and abiding love for Hodinöhsö:ni' narrative, community, ways of knowing, artistic expression, and embattled resistance in the face of the settler colonial project. I write from a space of profound investment in Hodinöhsö:ni' perspectives and histories surrounding wampum belts, treaties, our original agreements, and our commitment to the earth and all the entities acknowledged in the Thanksgiving Address. As with my previous study of Dakota texts, pictographs, story, and epistemology, I imagine this current tome to be another investigation into tribal theory, one intimated in its tiniest seeds and spores in *Tribal Theory in Native American Literature*. In this undertaking, I consider how a select array of Hodinöhsö:ni' writers, directors, and artists—a few stars in a multitude of Iroquois constellations—engage and conceptualize wampum traditions—oral, visual, and otherwise—as a way of organizing narrative and theoretically undergirding the aesthetics and poetics of their creations.

Writing now as a person of Seneca descent about Six Nations narrative, literary and diplomatic traditions, and visual literacies, I know myself to be not *longhouse*, by which I mean those with matrilineal descent raised on-territory and within the ceremonial cycle of the year, but as an active participant in the larger tradition of intellectual contentiousness that is *of the longhouse people* and their ways of inhabiting spaces, places, and institutions of higher learning. *Nya:weh* for pausing to read a few pages, perhaps even an entire chapter or the book in its entirety, and for taking time to consider with me how contemporary Hodinöhsö:ni' authors, artists, and filmmakers—none of these roles are necessarily fully distinct or separate from the other—engage the systems of Iroquois visual code and extend the rafters in our epistemological practices to bring forth the coming generations of Hodinöhsö:ni' citizens and descendants who will *teach us* through living and learning in their own unique ways, always dependent upon what came before and always further innovating our practices and survival strategies.

A Community of Iroquois Artists Reading the Wampum

The focus of this book is wampum and the role it has played and continues to play in Hodinöhsö:ni' collective memory, thought, epistemology, aesthetics, narrative, history, protocol, and treaty rights. Wampum belts are intrinsically linked to Hodinöhsö:ni' visual code, and their aesthetic engagements serve as extensions of the ideas recorded in purple and white shell. Further, wampum composes a significant portion of what we understand as Iroquois visual code, a set of mutually understood symbols and images that communicate culturally-embedded ideas to the viewer; these symbols arise from traditional forms such as pottery, beadwork, wampum, and sculpture and are contemporarily applied in media as varied as painting, film, metalsmithing, and digital displays.

Preeminent curator Ryan Rice (Mohawk) writes that "the unique iconography of wampum finds its way into many Iroquois artists' work, establishing a dialogue based on metaphors that preserve, understand, as well as question conformity."[1] Wampum belts, beadwork, ribbonwork, quilting, cornhusk dolls, masks, pottery, leatherwork, painting, sculpture, film, photography, literature, multimedia works, and other traditional and contemporary art forms engage and reconfigure Iroquois symbols, and in so doing, they comment upon the contexts within which Hodinöhsö:ni' intellectual production has arisen both pre- and post-contact; further, through their engagement of these forms, these visual narratives draw on the wellsprings of Hodinöhsö:ni' epistemology and cultural production. In a pragmatic way, Hodinöhsö:ni' artists, authors, and storytellers who engage these symbols in wampum specifically recall the original instructions encoded in cultural belts, allude to prophecies recorded, rearticulate their guiding wisdom, provide political commentary on treaty belts that record agreements with settler governments, and continue to honor Hodinöhsö:ni' commitment to these nation-to-nation compacts by reciting their record in a wide range of media. These new narratives are manifestations of what Neal Keating has observed as the "significant cultural continuity between contemporary Haudenosaunee people and their precolonial and colonial-era ancestors."[2]

Wampum belts are fundamentally related to other records of Iroquois visual code, and they have an intrinsically politically-charged content, as wampum belts were the method that Hodinöhsö:ni' chiefs and clanmothers used to record international diplomacy and treaty agreements initially with tribal nations and thereafter with settler governments as well. I am interested both in wampum belts that record cultural knowledges (i.e., Three Sisters Belt, Everlasting Tree Belt, Adoption Belt) and political agreements (i.e., Two Row Wampum, Canandaigua Treaty Belt, Wolf Belt), because both bodies of wampum belts carry knowledges that have politically and culturally significant applications to the challenges that face Hodinöhsö:ni' peoples today. I am not thus concerned with delving into the spiritual engagement of wampum and will seek to focus primarily upon secular analyses of wampum teachings, though I recognize that, as in all things Hodinöhsö:ni', the parts of a whole entity cannot be entirely separated, nor should they be. Instead, I will simply place my focus on the secular aspects of wampum, allowing others who are more knowledgeable—such as Tuscarora Faithkeeper, artist, and cultural historian Richard W. Hill Sr.—to discuss the ritual aspects of wampum.[3]

What are wampum belts? They are woven strands of white and purple/black tubular beads first made from whelk and quahog clamshells, respectively, or freshwater mussel shells; the beads were originally strung on hemp cords.[4] Ron Welburn writes that "roanoke (mussel) shell is the southern counterpart to wampum (quahog clam) shells, bushels of them being offered or given in transactions, or strings of either handed over in diplomatic exchanges to signify rhetorical affirmation."[5] In Hodinöhsö:ni' oral traditions, wampum was originally received by Ha:yëwënta' when he lay deep in grief at the side of Tully Lake. Ha:yëwënta' had quickly lost his three daughters and his wife to illness and accident in a shocking series of events, and he no longer wanted to carry on living. As he lay on the beach in grief, a large body of birds that had been floating on the waters of the lake arose in flight, and the tremendous force of so many wings drove the water from the lake, revealing the wampum shells on the floor of the lake. Ha:yëwënta' picked up the shells and strung them onto cord, repeating to himself "This would I do if I found anyone burdened with grief even as I am. I would take these shell strings in my hand and console them. The strings would become words and lift away the darkness with which they are covered. Holding these in my hand, my words would be true."[6] Ha:yëwënta' was able to clear his troubled mind and recover from the tremendous loss of his family, thereby allowing him to function as a speaker for the Peacemaker and to bring the message of peace and power to the Hodinöhsö:ni' peoples. His inspiration by wampum and its resulting revelations also created a means by which grieving peoples could assuage their grief without further suffering on their own part or necessitating a "mourning war" to return with captives to take the place of those lost.

This story from the Hodinöhsö:ni' second epoch illustrates the tremendous power of wampum to clear individuals' ears, eyes, and throats of negativity and to restore the Good Mind.[7] Wampum belts possess a personal and communal power for Hodinöhsö:ni' peoples that is specific to their cultural matrix; however, this power was very early recognized and intentionally undermined by settler authorities who sought to promote cultural genocide. To be specific, in the 1800s both the US and Canadian governments waged campaigns to steal (or acquire through other illicit means) the wampum belt collections of the Iroquois Confederacy on both sides of the border; in fact, the possession of wampum by Hodinöhsö:ni' peoples was outlawed under New York State's "Wampum Law," or section 27 of the New York State Indian Law (1899).[8] This program was undertaken in an effort to rob the Hodinöhsö:ni' of their intellectual traditions and political power; because the belts functioned as mnemonic records passed from keeper to keeper, the theft of the belts served to disrupt the process of intellectual transmission, thereby divesting the Hodinöhsö:ni' of the records of their intellectual and political self-determination. The campaign was temporarily successful and worked hand-in-hand with the establishment of residential and boarding schools that sought to eradicate

Ogwe'ëweh languages and histories and replace them with English, Christianity, and Eurocentric narratives and worldviews.

By 1900, hundreds of wampum belts were held in non-Native institutions including the State Museum of New York and the Smithsonian Institution and by individual collectors such as John Boyd Thacher, the mayor of Albany. Further, in 1924, the remaining wampum belts of the Confederacy in Ohsweken were confiscated by the RCMP as part of an effort to force a band council-style government on the people of Grand River.[9] These incidents of theft were acts of international aggression, as outlined by Richard W. Hill Sr.; similarly, I argue that they were crimes against humanity on par with the Spanish campaign to burn the libraries that recorded Mayan and Aztec spiritual, cultural, and scientific knowledges.[10]

The historical record indicates that non-Native contemporaries at the time understood the intellectual weight the wampum symbolized, carried, and communicated. For example, in an obituary for Chief Thomas Webster (Onondaga), wampum keeper for the Iroquois Confederacy, on July 9, 1897, Henry Edward Krehbiehl, music critic and writer for the *New-York Tribune*, notes with horror that upon the death of Chief Webster, it was discovered that nearly all of the wampum belts in his possession were missing, including the famed Ha:yëwënta' Belt.[11] Onondagas have traditionally held and cared for the wampum of the Six Nations, and these belts most likely would have been originals, though Krehbiehl, citing Horatio Hale, claims they were copies.[12] The *New-York Tribune* writer reflects, "Messengers have been sent to the various tribes to announce the death of Chief Webster and to call a condoling council to raise a chief and keeper of the wampum—that is, what is left of it."[13] Krehbiehl elaborates at length upon the role of wampum and Horatio Hale's efforts to catalogue wampum usage, and he analyzes a now-famous photograph of Six Nations chiefs reading the wampum and provides a detailed recounting of the basics of reading wampum according to John Buck.

Krehbiehl's extensive discussion of wampum's role and of Hale's efforts to document it aver his understanding of the irreplaceable significance the stolen belts possessed; his inclusion of the portrait of Grand River chiefs reading the wampum clearly indicates he understood that the knowledges held therein were carried from generation to generation

1. Grand River chiefs reading the wampum to Horatio Hale on September 14, 1871. Seated left to right are Hahriron Joseph Snow (Onondaga), Deyonhehgon George H. M. Johnson (Mohawk), Skanawatih John Buck (Onondaga), Sakayenkwaraton John Smoke Johnson (Mohawk), Kawenenseronton Isaac Hill (Onondaga), and Kanonkeredawih John Seneca Johnson (Seneca). Courtesy of the National Museum of the American Indian, Smithsonian Institution, catalog number PO9784. Photograph by NMAI Photo Services.

in their visual code. Krehbiehl laments that "[i]t does not seem probable that a single belt was left when the Onondaga towns were pillaged in 1779."[14] Perhaps Krehbiehl underestimates the value of the belts and the extremes to which Onondagas might go to preserve them, or perhaps he fully understood the extent of the willful plundering that Onondaga Territory was subject to during this time.

Given economic strictures and racist policies spanning the nineteenth and twentieth centuries, Hodinöhsö:ni' communities were unable to begin reclaiming these belts until the advent of the civil rights era with its concomitant groundswell of publicly visible activism. In the 1960s, Sakokwenionkwas Tom Porter with the White Roots of Peace, a Hodinöhsö:ni' activist organization, made efforts to reclaim belts held in Albany at the State Archives. In 1975, Richard W. Hill Sr. helped rematriate several thousand wampum beads held by the Buffalo and Erie County Historical Society to the Onondaga Nation. In 1983, several wampum belts held in the United States were repatriated to the Onondaga Nation, the first officially recognized act of repatriation, though individual small museums had voluntarily come forward in the 1960s to return belts, and the first incident of the rematriation of wampum belts occurred in Canada in 1988.[15] To date, hundreds of belts in the United States and Canada have been returned to the Confederacy through the efforts of individuals like Richard S. Hill Sr., Oren Lyons, and Elizabeth Montour. Numerous wampum belts, however, still remain in museums and private collections and await repatriation to the Confederacy.[16]

The various efforts, individual and institutional, to steal or otherwise illicitly acquire Hodinöhsö:ni' wampum belts stands as a definitive example of the violation not only of the sanctity of Indigenous knowledge practices, but also the desire to disrupt and control Native stories and understandings of self. Contrary to the appropriation and abuse of wampum belts outlined above, there are specific and detailed protocols for the handling and reading of wampum belts within the Iroquois Confederacy. For instance, wampum belts can only be taken out during the day in the sunlight; they are to be handled in a specific way in the longhouse (i.e., laid out on the floor in a circle on a white mat, or held on an upright stick for the purposes of reading them). Violations of these procedures have serious spiritual and social ramifications for the individuals responsible for their mishandling and misuse.

In her groundbreaking essay, "Wampum as Hypertext: An American Indian Intellectual Tradition of Multimedia Theory and Practice," Angela Haas examines the means by which wampum beads and belts function as historical and cultural record and also explores their significance to American Indian Studies scholars as well as to multimedia and literary studies experts. She writes:

> In order to memorize the belt and its story, the trained individual would impress in the mind the visual representation of the belt and

subsequently forge mnemonic associations between the visual representation of the belt and the accompanying story. Thus the wampum "reader" or presenter can trace the nodes of information and can link their associated inherited knowledge by tracing the embedded stories "told" by wampum and sinew hypertext. . . .

Wampum belts signify a surviving intellectual tradition that communicates living stories of a living culture. The treaties (and other messages woven into the wampum) are renewed by regularly revisiting and re-"reading" wampum vis-à-vis community memory and performance.[17]

Haas cogently argues for an understanding of wampum as an early form of hypertext, one which mnemonically records nodes of political agreements confirmed by consensus and activated in the memory of those who held them. Her examination also testifies to the sophistication and power of wampum traditions and illuminates the motivations to seek to interrupt and claim by right of conquest these records of Indigenous knowledges.

In many ways, the engagement of wampum imagery and narrative by contemporary Hodinöhsö:ni' authors furthers the rematriation of their wisdom and their epistemic record. Richard W. Hill Sr. writes of the alienation of generations of Hodinöhsö:ni' peoples from their cultural patrimony, staring through museum glass at wampum belts that were no longer held in ritual practice and witnessing the deaths of the carriers of oral tradition and wampum protocol during the ensuing fights to rematriate these belts to the Onondaga wampum keepers. By engaging wampum belts and their specific knowledges, Hodinöhsö:ni' authors, artists, and filmmakers enact a recovery of the wampum and the stories they hold; these culture workers return to the belts because they form a central portion of Hodinöhsö:ni' visual code and their rearticulation and renaming ensures the survival and flourishing of Ogwe'ëweh peoples.

The present volume is the first study of Hodinöhsö:ni' visuality, aesthetics, material culture, and print culture to focus on these subjects through the lens of wampum imagery and narrative in the literary and creative works of four contemporary Iroquois intellectuals: James Thomas Stevens (Mohawk), Eric Gansworth (Onondaga), Shelley Niro (Mohawk), and Tracey Deer (Mohawk). These artists, authors, and filmmakers overtly and subtly work with received traditions of Hodinöhsö:ni' knowledges, specifically wampum belts and their associated oral traditions, and their reinterpretations of these wampum belts, both treaty belts and cultural record belts, innovate and revitalize extant Hodinöhsö:ni' traditions. Further, by addressing and depicting these belts, they also reclaim and recuperate "lost" knowledges, as well as comment upon the relevance and continuity of nation-to-nation relations codified in wampum. This study considers the implications of their engagements of these traditions in the multiple media they employ for present and future Hodinöhsö:ni' intellectuals and community members, and the larger scholarly audiences engaged in the work of American studies, Indigenous studies, and gender and sexuality studies. I ground my analyses in crucial comparisons of readings of wampum in visual and print texts; each reading is situated in its own unique discursive field (i.e., wampum belt) and with its own attendant implications. The belts I orient my critical readings around are both cultural and diplomatic records. The cultural belts predate contact with non-Natives and include the Women's Nomination Belt and the Adoption (or Ransom) Belt. The Women's Nomination Belt codifies the rights of the clanmothers to appoint and depose chiefs, to hold clan names, and to control decision-making over war. The Adoption Belt was used ritually in the adoption of a non-Hodinöhsö:ni' individual into a nation and clan; the adoptee would become a full-fledged member of the adopting family and would often stand in for a recently deceased family member. This process allowed for the cycle of condolence to be completed and the release of grief attendant upon that loss. The treaty belts I examine include the Two Row Wampum and the Canandaigua Treaty Belt. The Two Row Wampum records the first treaty agreement between the Five Nations and non-Natives; it dates from a seventeenth-century treaty meeting between the Hodinöhsö:ni' and the Dutch and pledges perpetual friendship between the two parties involved. Specifically, the Two Row Wampum depicts the Hodinöhsö:ni' in a canoe and the Dutch in a ship sailing down the river of life with each group retaining their own language, culture, spirituality, and ways of being and not forcing their beliefs on the other group. The Canandaigua Treaty Belt (1794) records a pivotal treaty made between the Six Nations and the newly formed United States, and it is a friendship belt that depicts the thirteen colonies as figures holding hands with two Hodinöhsö:ni' figures beside a longhouse in the center of the belt. This treaty is the basis for many of the assertions of rights related to taxation and gambling that are currently being articulated by Hodinöhsö:ni' peoples in New York State. Taken collectively, these belts provide a methodological apparatus for reading each of the print and visual texts that engage them in the study that follows.

In chapter one, I consider James Thomas Stevens's *A Bridge Dead in the Water* and its poetic portrayal of the Two Row Wampum through a theoretical lens Stevens refers to as *(dis)Orientation*, which is constituted by a queering of the colonial relationship and its possessory language. I argue first that the effect of Stevens's strategy, a (dis)Orientation from a dismissal of Native knowledge to a (re)Orientation toward Indigenous narratives based in wampum and oral traditions, is an affirmation of the epistemic ties to Hodinöhsö:ni' political thought and its aesthetic expression in narrative. Secondly, I contend that the centrality of the Two Row philosophy to Stevens's poems in this collection innovates and rearticulates Hodinöhsö:ni' literary traditions through queering the colonial relationship and contemporary understandings of the Two Row Wampum itself. This rearticulation allows for the creation of a politically alive cultural relativism on the page, one that demands the recovery of historical memory *and* restitution and questions heteronormative framings of geography and possession. My reading holds Indigenous perspectives on treaties close in hand: print narratives of treaties are only one side's record of what Europeans believed or desired to have transpired, not necessarily the agreement reached in treaty council. I highlight Stevens's awareness of Hodinöhsö:ni' understandings of the law and of the interrelations and collisions of print, wampum, and oral treaty records in my reading of his poem *Alphabets of Letters*. Specifically, Stevens's representations of slippage in language and intent in colonial expressions and resulting deception or deviation from original agreements, such as the Two Row Wampum, exposes how colonial discourses pervade, deceive, and confuse stories, leaving Indigenous narrative scattered within its disordering rationale. More than mere reiterations of cultural expressions, Stevens's poems have pertinence and applicability to contemporary Hodinöhsö:ni' struggles for the land, as shown in his use of a Two Row poetic praxis in "Malaria," which yokes land theft to a discourse of equivalences, or seeming binary opposition, that results in dispossession.

Chapter two focuses on the role of the Canandaigua Treaty Belt and other friendship belts in works of fiction, poetry, drama, and memoir by Eric Gansworth, especially his 2004 novel *Smoke Dancing*, which portrays the tobacco and gasoline trade at Tuscarora. As a foundational document in Hodinöhsö:ni' treaty rights, the Canandaigua Treaty was intended to vouchsafe a range of Six Nations sovereign rights, including the right to hunt and fish in ceded territories, a right which was omitted in the English print version of the agreement signed by George Washington and ratified by Congress. Nonetheless, the Treaty of Canandaigua, or Pickering Treaty, remains the basis for Hodinöhsö:ni' rights to tax exemption for businesses on Native land and for the more general exercise of sovereign rights in the past and present. Gansworth portrays the contemporary challenges surrounding applications of the Canandaigua Treaty to the tobacco trade, especially problematic actions taken by clanmothers and chiefs in an era of increasing Christianization and corruption. The novel also succinctly articulates both the struggles against outside cultural forces (i.e., Christianity, capitalism) and against economic stresses of grinding poverty imposed by federal policy. Neither cultural hegemony nor impoverishment are naturalized in *Smoke Dancing*; their origins and intended effects in federal policy are sketched in concise detail, allowing no misattribution of the causality of this suffering, originating in settler abuses, to Tuscarora actors.

In his poetic memoir, *A Half-Life of Cardiopulmonary Function*, Gansworth again uses the implied presence and prevailing truths of the Canandaigua Treaty to enact a political and economic critique of the larger American society. Friendship chains function in this collection in a number of intersecting ways. First, they connect the human figures found in wampum to naturalistically parallel related individuals (represented through cornhusk dolls) to wampum friendship chains; and second, they portray a Hodinöhsö:ni' requickening over generations through the friendship chain. Finally, in multiple nuanced depictions, Gansworth uses friendship chains to signify the Canandaigua Treaty Belt itself, and its

specific international implications, and thus to provide a political and economic critique of the larger American settler society. The chapter closes
with a discussion of Gansworth's play, *Rabbit Dance*, in which he again
highlights the ongoing relationship of past treaties and current contexts,
in this instance, the Porter Agreement, which was established after the
War of 1812, to continuing struggles over Tuscarora international trade
rights. In this instance, specifically, he deals with the question of Tuscarora women's rights to vend beadwork at Niagara Falls. In portraying
friendship belts and the Canandaigua Treaty Belt in fiction, poetry, memoir, drama, and paintings, Gansworth emphasizes the role of wampum
in Hodinöhsö:ni' narrative and its centrality to the unique characteristics
that continue to define Hodinöhsö:ni' cultures across generations.

In chapters three and four, my endeavor is *tribal feminist* (Hodinöhsö:ni'-
specific) and *red feminist* (transnational) readings of filmic works by Shelley
Niro and Tracey Deer. Feminism historically has been a fraught term in
Native North American communities; its primary critique has been that it
serves the purposes of Euro-American and Euro-Canadian women without speaking specifically to Indigenous women's concerns.[18] In *Indigenous
Women and Feminism*, Shari Huhndorf and Cheryl Suzack acknowledge
this as "the oppositional logic between Indigenous feminism and struggles
for sovereignty," but emphasize "the need to address the urgent social, economic, and political problems confronting Indigenous women."[19] A host of
scholars, including Andrea Smith, Patricia Penn Hilden, Lee Maracle, Paula
Gunn Allen, Janet McAdams, Kim Anderson, Rebecca Tsosie, Laura Don-
aldson, and Kathryn Shanley, has identified the colonial legacy of enforced
heteropatriarchy upon tribal communities as a central scar of colonization
that urgently needs redress. In chapter three, I engage a Hodinöhsö:ni'-
specific tribal feminist rematriation of the Lynx, or Mother of Nations, in
the Gayaneshä'go:wah epic; I use this term, as the project is situated around
issues of reclamation of women's power in a Hodinöhsö:ni' context.[20] Contrastively, I situate my reading of the Adoption Belt in Tracey Deer's *Club
Native* as a red feminist intervention, owing to the transnational relevance
of Deer's decolonization of membership to the larger context of Canadian
settler-Indigenous relations and settler colonial studies.[21]

In chapter four, I focus upon Shelley Niro's contemporary portrayal of the Peacemaker/Ha:yëwënta'/Mother of Nations epic in the feature-length film *Kissed by Lightning* (2009), and I examine its relationship to the Women's Nomination Belt, and oral traditions of the Great Law, especially John Arthur Gibson's Onondaga version, which originates at Six Nations, Niro's home reserve. Placing the film and its emplotment in direct conversation with Hanni Woodbury's translation of Gibson's text, I examine the prominence Niro affords to the Mother of Nations, who was the first person to accept the Great Law, and the gender reversal of Tadodahoh, who is played by the figure of Kateri in the film. I argue that Niro provides a rearticulation of the Great Law that emphasizes women's role as part of a tribal feminist project, which is grounded in Hodinöhsö:ni' women's traditions. The chapter analyzes how Niro provides a filmic version of the oral retelling of the Great Law, which figuratively reads the Women's Nomination Belt wampum through the prominence of the Mother of Nations and the casting of Tadodahoh, the Onondaga chief, as a woman. The significance of this theoretical endeavor is that Niro's film re-presents women's experiences as normative in Hodinöhsö:ni' worldview, an assertion that is emic to Hodinöhsö:ni' culture. Yet women's centrality sometimes falls victim to the countervailing dominant culture and associated acculturating forces, as discussed by Michelle Raheja, Andrea Smith, Patricia Penn Hilden, and other scholars. By asserting women's central function in exercises of sovereignty (i.e., nomination), Niro reclaims Hodinöhsö:ni' women's power and importance for Hodinöhsö:ni' women themselves in the present and for future generations who will view the film. The visual affirmation of women's political roles extends and supports Hodinöhsö:ni' women and clanmothers' roles in occupations at sites like Ganienkeh, Oka, and Kanonhstaton (Caledonia). The implications of Niro's film for understanding and evaluating treaty agreements, such as the various Buffalo Creek treaties, one of which involved clanmothers as signatories (1788), and later corrupt treaties (1838, 1842) that omitted clanmother signatures and coerced the signatures of a mere handful of chiefs who were not representative of the Confederacy, are tremendous because Niro's reading of the Women's Nomination Belt situates clanmothers' prominence and traditional rights in the present and narrativizes how the reclamation of those powers in the present is necessary to the very survival of Hodinöhsö:ni' peoples in order to circumvent infighting and self-destruction from colonial grief.

In chapter four, I examine recent filmic works, both documentary and fictional, by Mohawk director Tracey Deer, including *Mohawk Girls* (2005 and 2009), *Club Native* (2008), and *Escape Hatch* (2009), which focus upon the struggles of Mohawk women vis-à-vis, broadly, cultural pressures to "marry in" and, more specifically, the 2004 Kahnawake Membership Law, which reiterates aspects of the Indian Act (1876). Selecting pivotal moments and directorial strategies from each of these documentary and fictional films, I delineate Tracey Deer's filmmaking as reflective of Hodinöhsö:ni' feminist praxis and red feminist intervention.

Continuing my focus on the importance of wampum, I situate that theoretical orientation in the long relationship of Mohawk women's art and literature to the Adoption Belt and other women's wampum belts that record these traditions and affirm women's centrality to social and political structure. In *Club Native*, Deer's voiceover at the film's beginning informs the audience that in the pre-contact era, in the longhouse an individual's nation and clan were reckoned by her mother's identity with *no reference to blood quantum*—and that Hodinöhsö:ni' people regularly practiced adoption of outsiders, both Native and non-Native. Meanwhile, recent applications of the Kahnawake Membership Law by the Council of Elders have, in fact, replicated the Indian Act's investment in blood quantum as a measure for Indian identity, and this emphasis upon blood quantum clearly excludes cultural and community affinity/identity, and adoption (in the absence of matrilineal descent), as standards for band membership. I contend that the body of Deer's work on Kahnawake Mohawk women's experience and her personal activism in tribal meetings, women's group, and editorship of *The Eastern Door*, a Kahnawake newspaper, constitute a vital intellectual contribution to decolonization and recovery from intergenerational trauma: Deer's filmic, journalistic, and activist work figuratively re-reads and re-quickens the Adoption Belt in order to insist upon humane, pragmatic, and creative constructions of Kahnawake Mohawk identity in response to colonization.

In the conclusion, I consider the local and broader implications of this study for the narratives held in wampum belts and those Hodinöhsö:ni' intellectuals who reclaim, innovate, and comment upon them. In particular, I suggest how the pragmatic orientation of works by Gansworth and Deer make specific, material, and localized contributions to larger decolonization movements and to the further affirmation and development of Hodinöhsö:ni' cultural traditions. I also consider how wampum belts, such as the Women's Nomination Belt, the Adoption Belt, the Two Row Wampum, and the Canandaigua Treaty Belt, continue to have political and cultural applications in contemporary settings. Finally, I speculate on the pragmatic impact of visual art that retells and affirms traditions that are tribally specific *and* pertinent to the international policy formation of the United States and Canada. I conclude by examining the legacy of Ray Fadden (Akwesasne Mohawk), a schoolteacher and museum curator who revived wampum traditions through interviewing elders and employing the belts as teaching tools at the Akwesasne Freedom School (and later the Six Nations Indian Museum). Fadden trained a generation of authors, storytellers, and political leaders, including Tom Porter, Doug George, Kay Olan, Maurice Kenny, and many others, and his legacy promises to continue as the museum collection is relocated to the Hiawatha Institute for Indigenous Knowledge, a national center for Indigenous knowledge that involves many of the same individuals he taught at Akwesasne. Fadden's extensive work with wampum illustrates why these records are so vital to Hodinöhsö:ni' epistemology, narrative, and international relations, and suggests why they are relevant to broader discussions of Indigenous knowledge, worldview, and politics.

The study that follows provides one potential model for using Indigenous story, narrative, and record as the basis for reclaiming and reenacting the original political agreements created between Native and settler nations. Wampum belts function as records in widely varying contexts, insofar as these belts record international agreements, key historical events, and original instructions from various epochs of Iroquois history. Their engagement by these artists represents a reclamation of Indigenous wisdom and narratives on Indigenous terms, acts that function as decolonizing recovery in a context where settlers far outnumber Indigenes. The force and power inherent in claiming this wampum wisdom after centuries of forced acculturation and cultural genocide are breathtaking, and it portends immense transformation in the generations to come.

I would be remiss if I did not expressly state that the work that follows represents solely one individual's perspective on Hodinöhsö:ni' visual code, and within this monograph, I always seek to honor the political integrity of the Hodinöhsö:ni' communities from which these works hail and which they depict. The artists and authors whose work I study are claiming these Indigenous materials (i.e., wampum images and their narratives) on sovereign terms to create Indigenous representations and tell Indigenous stories that honor their communities. As someone who is of Seneca descent (patrilineal descent), I acknowledge that I stand outside this circle of tribal sovereignty, as a non- Hodinöhsö:ni' citizen, with a sympathetic eye to analyzing the impact these works have on their various audiences, Native and non-Native, and their implications for future generations, Native and non-Native.[22]

We live in an age of prophesied events coming to fruition: the changes predicted by the Peacemaker, Handsome Lake, and other Iroquois spiritual leaders now unfold around us. Hodinöhsö:ni' peoples continue to assert their unique identity and sovereign status in acts like the occupation at Kanonhstaton, the Iroquois Nationals lacrosse team's insistence upon using Hodinöhsö:ni' passports, and the reclamation of Mohawk Territory by Roger Jock and the People of the Way of the Longhouse at Akwesasne. The Idle No More movement sparked in late 2012 and has shown an impressive globalizing and alliance-building potential, one that promises to fundamentally alter Kanata as we know it. In a hemispheric context, the growing population of Nahua speakers north of the US-Mexico border presages the predominance of that language in North America in another 500 years, if Leslie Marmon Silko's prediction is correct.[23] In a global context even the most recalcitrant settler governments, such as Australia and the United States, have signed the United Nations Declaration of Indigenous Peoples Rights. Everywhere around us there are markers of the resurgence of Indigenous peoples movements and the recognition of that growth by settler citizens and governments. The reclamation of wampum, not just from the museum, but in the day-to-day cultural production of Hodinöhsö:ni' peoples stands as a signal example of all that was not, in fact, lost in the conquest of the Americas. The narrative of utter cultural destruction that is a function of settler nostalgia is disproved by the reclamation of Indigenous practices like wampum and its reading and by the restoration of Native language, as evidenced by the rebirth of previously "dead" languages like Myaamia and Wampanoag.[24] It is impossible to predict what possibilities will be unleashed by this renewal of Indigenous culture and knowledge; however, the coming generations will bear witness to these events which are hallmarks of the rebirth of Turtle Island and the birth of the next world, however literal or metaphoric, hereafter.

Acknowledgments

I am grateful to the artists, authors, and directors whose work provided inspiration for this book. Tracey Penelope Tekahentáhkhwa Deer, Eric Gansworth, Shelley Niro, and James Thomas Aronhióta's Stevens have all been incredibly generous with their time in discussing their work and responding to my own musings on their artistic production.

The initial drafting of this manuscript was supported in part by course releases generously provided by the University of Colorado (CU) at Boulder English Department and College of Arts and Sciences. The CU Graduate Center for the Arts and Humanities, the Eugene M. Kayden Award, and the Dean's Fund for Excellence provided further support with research awards for travel to Grand River Territory, Newtown at Cattaraugus Territory, Kahnawake Mohawk Territory, and Kanatsiohareke Traditional Mohawk Community. The Roser Visiting Artist Program funded an artist's residency and related exhibit of Shelley Niro's work, which assisted in the drafting of chapter three. The Kayden Award also covered costs associated with publication. Jennifer Shannon also took the lead in organizing the exhibit and surrounding events (film panels, film screenings, and so on). A small portion of chapter four appeared in an early form in "Gathering the Threads Together: Urban/Diasporic/Multitribal Native North American Narratives in Nationalist Theory," in *Comparative Indigeneities of the Américas: Toward a Hemispheric Approach*, edited by M. Bianet Castellanos, Lourdes Gutiérrez Nájera, and Arturo J. Aldama, University of Arizona Press (Kelsey 2012).

I am thankful to the many scholars who were generous with their time in either reading drafts of particular chapters or in providing specific feedback on resources I should take under consideration. Thanks to Chadwick Allen, Danika Medak-Saltzman, Carol Miller, and Teresa Toulouse for your thorough readings and detailed feedback. Thanks to CU's Native American Indian Studies (NAIS) faculty for providing feedback on the Canandaigua Treaty Belt chapter. Thanks to Nicholle Dragone for insights into the Good Mind and introducing me to Deborah Doxtator's scholarship. Thanks to Rick Hill and Chandra Maracle for providing inspiration throughout the conception and revision of this book, and thanks to Darren Bonaparte for timely humor.

I would like to specifically thank Virve Wiland of the Woodlands Cultural Centre Library and Andrea Kaniehtenhawi Meloche, Tracey Deer's personal assistant, for their help in tracking down articles and cultural experts. Tammy Beauvais, Alex McComber, Timmy Norton, and Patty Bush Stacey, all Kahnawake Mohawk citizens with professional and community accolades that would be impossible to enumerate in this brief space, were tremendously generous in sharing sage insights in *Club Native* and in granting permission to use their images in this volume.

I am thankful to my family for providing the inspiration that led me to this topic. Thanks to my grandfather Bill Kelsey, my parents Charles and Vicki Kelsey, and my siblings Marianne and Chester Kelsey; thanks to my maternal grandmother Lois Shiffler Bollinger and the generations of women from whom I am descended. Thanks especially to Levi who knows best how the trials of manuscript preparation affect the real stuff of life: reading at basketball practice and the kitchen table, postponing hikes and trips to the bookstore, preparing and eating meals, and getting to bed on time.

I am grateful to my ancestors and others who came before me and hope I have honored their work and struggles in some small way, in addition to smoothing the path for the ones who will come after me and who will improve upon my work in ways that I could never foresee. I apologize in advance for any mistakes that were made in the creation of this book; my sole intention has been to enrich the conversations that are already happening in Hodinöhsö:ni' communities about our core knowledges and treaty agreements, and, where appropriate, to bring them into the larger discourse and debate of the academy. I am certain they have much to contribute to our understanding of contemporary Indigenous communities, ways of being/knowing, healing, survival, intergenerational trauma, and restorative justice.

Note on Language and Orthography

Throughout this study, I use the Seneca language, or *Onöndowa'ga:' gawënö'*, and the orthography employed by Phyllis Eileen Williams Bardeau in her Seneca language dictionary and books. Bardeau's *Definitive Seneca: It's in the Word* is my primary reference. In cases where the original text utilizes another *Hodinönohsö:ni' gawë:nö'* (language), I retain those spellings from the original text.

I make specific language choices to ensure gender-neutrality by alternately employing rematriation and repatriation.

Reading the WAMPUM

1

Two Row Wampum in James Thomas Stevens's
A Bridge Dead in the Water and *Tokinish*

Then, the White Man asked what symbol the Ogwého:weh would use as a symbol of what both parties are thinking. The Ogwého:weh said the way we would symbolize our agreement is that we Ogwého:weh have our Canoe, we will put everything we have in our Canoe (language, laws, beliefs, etc . . .). You (White People) also have your ship where your people, your beliefs, your languages, your laws shall be placed. Also between the Canoe and the Ship, we shall have rules of conduct between our peoples. Three principles shall be adhered to between our peoples. 1st—there will be everlasting peace, 2nd—we will maintain a good friendship, 3rd—we will always practice "the Good Mind" (which means mutual respect, justice, and equality). This is how long it is to last: as long as the sun is in motion in the sky. Also for as long as the rivers are flowing. Also for as long as grass is growing on the earth. It means that for as long as the Earth lasts, this is the law that we will follow between our peoples. And after the Dutch probably about one lifespan later, the English outnumbered them, and they took it over. And they said, we think that agreement is good that you made with the Dutch, we'd like also to make the agreement, so our ancestors made the same agreement with the English as well. And that's when it became an iron chain, and at some point later on after that, they said we'll make that iron silver now, because iron can rust. If we make it a silver chain between us, that'll never rust. We'll just have to keep it clean from time to time, and that means to resolve issues. So this is our method right here; this is our method of resolving issues between the Ogwého:weh and the government of the non-Natives.
                    —Leroy (Jock) Hill (Cayuga Nation Sub-Chief, Bear Clan)[1]

This chapter explores how James Thomas Stevens (Akwesasne Mohawk) dramatizes the need to honor the Two Row Wampum in his poetry collections, *A Bridge Dead in the Water* and *Tokinish*. While intended as an affirmation of equality, separation, and sovereignty, various settler governments have failed to honor the Two Row Wampum in a multitude of ways (e.g., the Indian Act, Major Crimes Act, American Indian Citizenship Act, Pick-Sloan Act, US Census). In this chapter, I suggest that Stevens's poetic embodiment of depredations against the Two Row dramatizes the tension between theory and praxis in making the cognitive leap from foundational treaties to their application in contemporary political contexts. This reading also focuses on James Thomas Stevens's use of queerness (or "two-spiritedness") as a focal point of sameness between colonizer and colonized from which to assert Indigenous sovereignties in physical bodies and geographic bodies.

Two Row Wampum: History, Background, and Cartography

Hodinöhsö:ni' oral tradition records the first treaty belt passed over the fire between Iroquois and Europeans as the Two Row Wampum or *Gaswënta'*.[2] This belt records a seventeenth-century agreement between the Iroquois and the Dutch; the Hodinöhsö:ni' Confederacy and Two Row Wampum Campaign allies celebrated the 400th anniversary of this treaty in 2013, as 1613 is the date generally identified for this treaty meeting on the Hudson in Iroquois oral tradition.[3] In "Indian Self-Government in the Haudenosaunee Constitution," Onondaga Faithkeeper Oren Lyons observes, "This particular treaty is important because it was established for all time the process by which we would associate with our white brethren."[4] Seneca artist and scholar G. Peter Jemison designates the Two Row Wampum as "the basis for all treaties."[5] The belt is comprised of two long parallel purple lines on a white belt, and the purple lines on a white background metaphorically record one of the most important ideas in Hodinöhsö:ni' political philosophy and international/settler relations. In essence, the two purple lines of shell stand for the Hodinöhsö:ni' and the Dutch. That these lines do not intersect and do not share a common origin is pivotal; simultaneously, the fact that they are both purple and fashioned of the same materials signifies recognition of a shared identity as humans. In this belt, the Hodinöhsö:ni' are informing the Dutch that as long as the Hodinöhsö:ni' remain in their canoe, and the Dutch in their ship, as long as the Hodinöhsö:ni' retain their own language, culture, government, and spirituality, and the Dutch their own language, culture, government, and religion, the two groups will be able to coexist peacefully. More specifically, as long as the Dutch do not force their way of life on the Hodinöhsö:ni' and as long as they concede the common ground (white) as Iroquois normative, the two will cohabitate in peace. In reading the Two Row Wampum, Oren Lyons states:

> The field of white represents peace and the river of life. We will go down this river in peace and friendship as long as the grass is green, the water flows, and the sun rises in the east.
>
> It is [in] this treaty that those famous words were spoken. You will note the two rows do not come together, they are equal in size, denoting the equality of all life and one end is not finished, denoting the ongoing relationship in the future. With this belt was the great Silver Covenant Chain of Friendship [given by the Dutch at the original treaty proceedings] that is mentioned throughout our interwoven histories.
>
> This is a great humanitarian document because it recognizes equality in spite of the small size of the White colony and insures safety, peace, and friendship forever, and sets the process up for all of our ensuing treaties up to this moment.[6]

The background of white in the belt signifies the Hodinöhsö:ni' and Dutch share common ground in the Great Peace (Gayaneshä'go:wa:h), and by creating a belt that represents the Dutch in the field of white, the Hodinöhsö:ni' are bringing the Dutch into their political economy and into their lands or territories: the belt is a map of the way that both groups will share the commons and conduct themselves in their shared territories. The Dutch have the right to live in Iroquoia so long as they abide by these basic laws of enjoying one's own unique way of life and not enforcing one's worldview upon other groups.

As the cultural relativism of Herman Meyndertsz Van Den Bogeart's contemporary account suggests, in some ways the Dutch were able to honor this treaty as well or better than some of their later European counterparts; perhaps this greater success in honoring the Two Row Wampum is predicated upon Dutch literacy in Hodinöhsö:ni' cartography and agreements in wampum.[7] While the Dutch would likely have had a copy of the Two Row Belt to honor the original treaty proceedings, and while the belt would have been ritually cleaned at each subsequent meeting, we have no established record that the later French and English settlers literally inherited the belt, though treaty proceedings published in European languages vouch that both of these groups did, in fact, metaphorically and politically inherit the Two Row, as Hodinöhsö:ni' hoyane:h (chiefs) continually reminded them. All Hodinöhsö:ni' agreements in subsequent treaties with the Dutch took this original treaty as their premise, and in all ensuing treaty deliberations with other European powers, the Hodinöhsö:ni' used the assumptions inherent in the Two Row as guiding principles.[8] In "Kaswentha," a report for the Royal Commission on Aboriginal Peoples, Paul Williams (Kayenasenh) and Curtis Nelson (Arihote) write:

> The Haudenosaunee have had more than three centuries of treaty relations with the Crown. Where other nations Indigenous to North America can point to one or two seminal "treaties" as the foundation and origins of their relations with the Crown, the Haudenosaunee have a continuum of evolving relations, contained in streams of principles and commitments, not in singular events or documents.
>
> The crucial relationships—the Silver Covenant Chain and the Two Row Wampum—were developed over time and reaffirmed so often that it is pointless to recite every instance.[9]

Nearly every treaty proceeding from the seventeenth century until the late nineteenth century begins with the European and Six Nations delegates reciting the principles of the Two Row and Covenant Chain and cleaning the chain of any rust or tarnish. As Williams and Nelson note, the Canadian (and US) authorities dropped their working knowledge of this part of the treaty around the turn of the twentieth century, while the Hodinöhsö:ni' have retained these original agreements as part of their international policy with Canada and the United States.[10]

The premise of this treaty is returned to continually in Hodinöhsö:ni' narrative, art, and culture; this treaty is commemorated orally, so distant in event that its actual date of creation is contested heavily in non-Native academic circles.[11] Hodinöhsö:ni' artists in numerous media bring the image of the Two Row into their works with regularity, from Shelley

2. Shelley Niro, "Grand River Promises." Reprinted with permission of the artist.

Niro's *Grand River* to Eric Gansworth's closing images in *A Half-Life of Cardiopulmonary Function*. Invoked at tribal gatherings and treaty commemorations to this day, the Two Row has a foundational role in shaping how Hodinöhsö:ni' peoples imagined themselves vis-à-vis Europeans in the past *and* how they imagine themselves vis-à-vis Euro-Americans, Euro-Canadians, and other settlers now. Williams and Nelson describe this remembrance of the Two Row and other treaties as marks of Hodinöhsö:ni' "consistency— the careful guarding and maintenance of a way of law and knowledge."[12] The treaty's fundamental caveat, that the settlers' culture was useful to settlers, but was not appropriate for the Hodinöhsö:ni', continues to influence matters as varied as mundane, lived philosophy (i.e., education, clothing, dress, and longhouse religious practices) to activist decolonization (i.e., land protection/reclamation at sites like Caledonia/Kanonhstaton and Ganienkeh).[13] The relative preoccupation with the Two Row in non-academic and academic Iroquois conversations also confirms this

3. Eric Gansworth, "Expiration," from *A Half-Life of Cardiopulmonary Function.*
Image © Eric Gansworth, used with permission.

foundational role in shaping and reflecting Hodinöhsö:ni' thought. For that reason, this essay incorporates the Two Row structure into its comparison of two collections of James Thomas Stevens's poetry: (1) *Tokinish*, which models European organization of knowledge through etymology, and (2) *A Bridge Dead in the Water*, which illustrates Hodinöhsö:ni' epistemic practices through a queer lens.

In essence, the Two Row is central to the history of Hodinöhsö:ni' treaties, to the political philosophy of the Ogwe'ëweh in nation-to-nation engagements, and to current land protections, reclamations, and settlements that are expressive of the larger political consciousness of the Hodinöhsö:ni'. Little wonder that Hodinöhsö:ni' artists, storytellers, writers, and politicians all return to the Two Row as a touchstone or a litmus test for evaluating all potential future actions. Through a re-envisionment of the Two Row in etymologic and cartographic poesis, James Thomas Stevens brings new insights into contemporary understandings of the Two Row Wampum and extends its teachings to speculate upon decolonial inclusions of queer Hodinöhsö:ni' identities.

James Thomas Stevens and Two Row Teachings

Illustrating the Gaswënta's pivotal influence in Hodinöhsö:ni' thought, Stevens theoretically engages a paradigm of (dis)Orientation and the Two Row philosophy in his most recent collection, *A Bridge Dead in the Water* (2007). The effect of Stevens's strategy of (dis)Orientation from a Western chauvinism and triumphal narrative and (re)Orientation to Indigenous cultural relativism and story is an affirmation of Hodinöhsö:ni' political thought and its ties to wampum teachings. This (dis)Orientation has a precursor in an earlier collection, *Tokinish*, which portrays how European systems of epistemic organization (i.e., Williams's *A Key into the Language of America*) disfigure and garble Indigenous narratives. Stevens's body of poetry, especially *Tokinish* and *A Bridge*, are undergirded by an engagement of the Two Row Wampum and its investment in the sanctity of Native claims to Turtle Island. The tension between settler and Indigenous ways of knowing is allegorized by the Gaswënta', which maps Hodinöhsö:ni' territory, and Ogwe'ëweh and settlers' agreed-upon place within it. Ultimately, Stevens's Native speakers invite the non-Native lover to map the queer

Indigenous body on its own terms through tropes of sexualized "location" and "charting;" thus, Stevens uses the Two Row through a LGBTQ2 lens to lay bare the colonial epistemic impulses that contest Hodinöhsö:ni' peoples' ability to enforce this treaty.[14]

James Thomas Stevens is an Akwesasne Mohawk who was born in Niagara Falls in 1966. He is one of several children; his brother Scott Stevens, former director of the D'Arcy McNickle Center, is noteworthy as another Indigenous academic. James Stevens studied at the School of Visual Arts, Brooklyn College, the Institute of American Indian Arts (IAIA), and the Naropa Summer Institute. While at IAIA, Stevens was a student of Arthur Sze; while at Naropa, he studied under Anne Waldman, Allen Ginsberg, Gary Snyder, and Anselm Hollo. Stevens later completed an MFA at Brown University, and he is the author of *Tokinish, Combing the Snakes from His Hair, (dis)Orient, Mohawk/Samoa: Transmigrations, The Mutual Life, Bulle/Chimère,* and *A Bridge Dead in the Water.* His *Notes on Music I Never Heard* was nominated for a Pushcart Prize in 1996, and he won the 2000 Whiting Writers Award for *Combing the Snakes from His Hair.* He was nominated for a Before Columbus/American Book Award in 2003, and he was a finalist for the National Poetry Series Award in 2005. He has held academic positions at Haskell Indian Nations University, SUNY Fredonia, and the Institute of American Indian Arts.

Stevens's collection *A Bridge Dead in the Water* treats an assemblage of topics, territories, and historical periods, from Jesuit China to mission-era Huronia and Iroquoia, from insurance plans and actuarial science to "Relationships, Colonization, and Other Accidents," and from eighteenth century primers for Mohawk children to the contemporary war for oil in Iraq. In a review of *A Bridge Dead in the Water,* Alan Gilbert writes that Stevens's collection "turns the notion of cultivated upside down, in the process exposing the barbarism it conceals. Ideas and directives concerning the proper care of the self and the environment don't arise in a vacuum, and one of the most striking aspects of Stevens's poetry is its complex layering of the personal and the historical."[15] The initial segment of this reading of *A Bridge Dead in the Water* will consider Stevens's technique of (dis)Orientation and geographies of desire in the opening poems of the collection as a way of queering the colonial encounter and exposing its assumptions of cultural superiority, and the second section of analysis will focus on Two Row philosophy and Two Spiritedness in *A Bridge Dead in the Water* and *Tokinish*.

It is worthy of mention that Stevens himself does not identify with the term Two Spirit, although he does identify his work as LGBTQ2; Stevens's critique of the term arises in response to a lack of clearly identifiable third gender traditions in Iroquoia, making Two Spirit a generalized term that possesses no Hodinöhsö:ni' equivalent.[16] I use queer and LGBTQ2 in this essay, because as Qwo-Li Driskill, Chris Finley, Brian Joseph Gilley, and Scott Lauria Morgensen write in the introduction to *Queer Indigenous Studies: Critical Interventions in Theory, Politics, and Literature*:

> We find both *queer* and *Two-Spirit* useful for a number of reasons. *Queer* carries with it an oppositional critique of heteronormativity and an interest in the ambiguity of gender and sexuality. *Two-Spirit* was proposed in Indigenous organizing in Canada and the United States to be inclusive of Indigenous people who identify as GLBTQ or through nationally specific terms from Indigenous languages. When linked, *queer* and *Two-Spirit* invite critiquing heteronormativity as a colonial project, and decolonizing Indigenous knowledges of gender and sexuality as one result of that critique.

Further, speaking of the history of the term's usage, they write that

> as Two-Spirit identity was cultivated and debated among Indigenous [LGBTQ2] people, it engendered new thought across the differences in urban and rural, traditional and nontraditional, academic and popular writing that showed *the term retained a capacity to do many forms of work.* [emphasis mine]

For these reasons, I acknowledge the productive intellectual histories that render *Two-Spirit* a liberatory term and the activist transformation it embodies, while tending toward LGBTQ2 and queer as terms both more capacious and reflective of the Hodinöhsö:ni' intervention in settler colonialisms that Stevens's poetry enacts.[17]

(dis)Orientation and Geographies of Desire

Originally published in 2005 as *(dis)Orient*, a chapbook, the first poem in the collection was inspired by Stevens's 2002 trip to China and a visit to the Catholic Xujiahui Cathedral, during which he was inspired to research Jesuit history in Asia, because of the similarities he found with Jesuit history in Iroquoia. The result was a poem that "addresses issues of charting and mapping, as well as issues of authority,"[18] and a narrative of colonization that eroticizes bodies of land and water, while (dis)Orienting the colonizer's gaze upon those same geographic and human bodies. Working directly with the original texts of the seventeenth- and eighteenth-century *Jesuit Relations*, letters written home from missions to the leaders of the Jesuit Order, the speaker of *(dis)Orient* examines the conflation of Asian and American Indian identities in such a way as to highlight the colonizer's confusion and the highly erotic nature of this confounder. The end result is a disentangling of American Indian (and Asian) narrative(s) from the Jesuit narrative of civilization and savagery, and a setting of the stage for applications of Two Row political and intellectual economies from historic to present contexts.

Queer, LGBTQ2, and Hodinöhsö:ni' methodologies are central to my readings of *A Bridge Dead in the Water* and *Tokinish*, and they are especially rich strategies for interrupting the business-as-usual processes of knowledge formations about colonized peoples. In the introduction to *Queer Indigenous Studies: Critical Interventions in Theory, Politics, and Literature*, Qwo-Li Driskill, Chris Finley, Brian Joseph Gilley, and Scott Lauria Morgensen invite

> scholars and activists to pay attention to the ways that heteronormativity—the normalizing and privileging of patriarchal heterosexuality and its gender and sexual expressions—undermines struggles for decolonization and sovereignty and buoys the powers of colonial governance. Current Indigenous national struggles must question and challenge their relation to [LGBTQ2] people. . . . [B]y disrupting colonially imposed and internalized systems of gender and sexuality, Indigenous queer and Two-Spirit critiques can move decolonizing movements outside dominant logics and narratives of "nation."[19]

Thus, LGBTQ2 methods make possible decolonial critiques that highlight the normalizing gaze of European heteronormativities, and in so doing, they access greater space for actualizing Indigenous sovereignty and community revitalization.[20] In *When Did Indians Become Straight?*, Mark Rifkin elaborates upon this potential:

> The critique of heteronormativity, then, can reveal both how U.S. control over native peoples is legitimized and naturalized by reference to the self-evident superiority of bourgeois homemaking and how native intellectuals and governments have sought to validate tribal autonomy through investments in native *straightness*.

Further, Rifkin observes:

> the pursuit of queer methods with a focus on native sovereignty highlights the ways the racialization of Indigenous peoples as Indians works in the [service] of delegitimizing modes of collectivity at odds with U.S. jurisdictional logics/claims, engaging in an antiracist project whose aim is opening additional room for self-representation by native polities.[21]

Clearly, the use of queer methodologies offers new potentials in decolonizing methodologies, and this essay will avail itself of those liberatory possibilities in a Hodinöhsö:ni'-specific context. This essay will perform a Two Row reading, which traces the origins of certain assumptions about Indigenous peoples and nationhood to their sources in European epistemic practice, as hinted at by Rifkin above and as articulated by Stevens in *Tokinish*, as well as (re)Orienting a second reading founded in Indigenous principles found in the Two Row that incorporates LGBTQ2 strategies.

(dis)Orient's narrative thread builds upon numerous voices, from the voice of an "undiscovered" Native "talking back" to the Jesuits' narrative of discovery to a multitude of actual Jesuit voices from the missions in Iroquoia, Huronia, and Asia (i.e., Lafitau, Albanel, Marquette).[22] The two epigraphs to *(dis)Orient* reveal the intellectual mechanism by which the speaker will lay bare the fallacies of the Jesuits' understanding of their encounters with Chinese and with American Indians, errors that are rooted in competing cartographies:

Meaning is revealed by the pattern formed and the light thus trapped—not by the structure, the carved work itself. (W. Bion, *A Memoir of the Future*)

At length all our journeyings, which were made only by paths all strewn with Crosses, came to an end very fittingly at a lake bearing the name of the Cross, from it's [sic] having the Perfect shape of one. (Fr. Albanel, *The Jesuit Relations*)

(dis)Orient's speaker lays bare the inaccurate projections and assumptions made by the Jesuits and other colonizers, as well as the pattern revealed and the stasis (i.e., "trapped" light) produced by strivings for meaning. The path strewn with crosses enacts the figurative blindness of the missionaries, given that Iroquoia and Huronia were cut throughout with paths from village to village, and the final enforcement of this marking of the land (i.e., crosses) is the vision of Lake Champlain as a lake formed in the shape of the cross.

The topically obvious thrust of this poem is the debunking of the Bering Land Bridge theory, which Stevens designates a "dead bridge" and a "dead theory" in his introduction. The poem's Indigenous speaker states, "Relating your stories, / I feel the irritable reaching, / looking steadily to your experience / till a pattern emerges," and this observation echoes Bion's assertion that "Meaning is revealed by the pattern formed and the light thus trapped."[23] The announcement of the death of Western theories of the relationship between the hemispheres of conquest in the collection's title, *A Bridge Dead in the Water*, immediately sets the tone for all of the poems to follow: "No making opposite shores connect, / the landbridge dead in the water. / If I name the rapid—La Chine / it does not bring China closer."[24] Stevens here illuminates the process by which creating maps, however inaccurate, and claiming territories, however inhabited, are entwined.

Stevens portrays the conflict between Indigenous and European cartographies throughout *A Bridge* as a way of affirming the necessity of the Two Row's separation of the lifeways: both approaches to mapping and knowledge are equal; in fact, the European mapping of North American lands is often patently wrong. A number of geographers have explored these same tensions within their discipline, most notably Margaret Wickens Pearce, Renee Pualani Louis, Jay Johnson, and Albertus Promano. Pearce and Louis describe Indigenous cartographies as

> diverse as Indigenous cultures, from Hawaiian performative cartographies to Navajo verbal maps and sand paintings and the Nuwuvi Salt Song Trail. Indigenous mapping may be gestural, chanted, or inscribed in stone, wood, wall, tattoo, leaf, or paper. Indigenous maps may be used to assess taxes, guide a pilgrim, connect the realms of the sacred and profane, or navigate beyond the horizon. Clearly, Indigenous cartographies are process oriented as opposed to product dependent. . . .
>
> Finally, Indigenous processual cartographies also differ from Western cartography in that they emphasize experienced space, or place, as opposed to the Western convention of depicting space as universal, homogenized, and devoid of human experience.[25]

The collision between these process- and object-oriented epistemological cartographies is portrayed as in constant conflict in *A Bridge* while simultaneously entwined with the language of sex and conquest. Jay Johnson, Pualani Louis, and Albertus Promano caution that "the technologies of Western cartography [are] . . . implicated in the European colonial endeavor," and Kelley and Francis observe that "the 'putting on record' always seems to accompany Indigenous loss of resources and the oral tradition itself."[26] For Stevens, this language of theft and conquest is inescapable, and he uses the twinning of queer sexuality and the Two Row to affirm the equality or sameness narrated by this wampum's teaching, while reading the belt to show the difficulty in honoring this treaty when the terms of relations are still couched in the colonial imaginary.[27] Furthermore, engaging Rikin's methodology of queering Indigenous nationhood makes possible a critique of settler colonialism in Stevens's *A Bridge*.

Stevens utilizes a myriad of Jesuit voices taken directly from the *Relations* to establish the settler disquiet at the original peoples and their territories, the desperate effort to organize a body of knowledge about Indigenes, and the profoundly colored lens that holds Asian and American Indians in that gaze, while seeking to chart their territories and to disavow their humanity. Beyond obvious articulations of cultural chauvinism, the excerpts from the *Relations* that Stevens interpolates throughout the poem highlight the specific blindness inherent in these records: from Father Dablon, "By glancing, as one can, at the Map of the lakes, one will gain more light upon all these missions than by long descriptions that might be given of them;" and from Father Albanel, "If the savages are to be believed, in one place, where the birds shed their feathers in molting time, any Savages or deer coming to the spot are buried in feathers over their heads, and are often unable to extricate themselves."[28] This lurching about for any organizing principle to understand the new societies encountered and, more importantly, to claim their territory seems a signal marker of the *Jesuit Relations*, and the poem's speaker highlights this desperate quest for familiarity. Similarly, the voices of European narratives of contact in *Notes on Music I Never Heard* reflect this frantic reaching to understand Native peoples within a European framework: *"Barbarians' . . . best music is said to be hideous and astonishing,"* and "The size of a tribe's characteristic step / was attributed to this factor: / *The narrower the step, the narrower the mind."*[29] The willingness to believe in fantastic scenes, such as places where humans choke in birds' feathers, and the devotion to simplifying difference within truisms linked to physiognomy (i.e., foot width and intelligence) illustrate an anxiety to situate perceived racial inferiors in a hierarchy where Europeans are assured rule.

The strategies that evolve to amass a body of knowledge about a given unconverted population level any differences beyond the affirmation of distinction from the European (i.e., civilized, Christian, literate in the Roman alphabet). This presumed sameness of identity between Asian and North American also reinforces the function of the land bridge theory to simplify much more complex origins, identities, and cultures, illustrating the failure of European cartography to accomplish equal specificity found in the Two Row Wampum and its reliance on oral recall and interpretation true to its original spirit in reading the wampum. Stevens places two excerpts from Jesuit letters in China and North America side by side, highlighting the strain to see North America through the previously established lens for Asia:

The little people who inhabit these shifting tenements, strike camp in the morning all together, to go fishing or work in the rice; they sow and they gather here three times a year . . . [.] One might say they are ready to embrace [our religion]; but he would be mistaken. They respond coldly: Your religion is nowhere in our books, it is a strange religion . . . [.] (Fr. De Prémare, *Lettres Edifiantes et Curieuses des Jesuites de Chine*)

The Indians gather and prepare [the rice] for food as follows. In the month of September, which is the proper time for the harvest, they go in canoes through these fields of wild rice and shake its ears into the canoe . . . [.] I told these Wild Rice People of my design to go and discover remote nations in order to teach them the mysteries of our holy religion . . . [.] They told me that I would meet nations who never show mercy to strangers, but break their heads for no reason . . . [.] (Fr. Marquette, *Recueil de voyages*[30])

These passages are separated by several decades and thousands of miles,[31] and yet, the Jesuit vision of potential converts is so universalizing that even *manoomin* is renamed as *rice* to force Asian and American Indians into the same category, which mirrors the European mapping process. Further, and more obviously, the presumption of the Jesuits to deliver their religion to the unconverted is unfailing across the continents and centuries. Yet, the poem's speaker articulates the falsity of this leveling gaze: "Orient or disorient. / Huronia & Cathay. / The landbridge will not be forced / to function / by what you find familiar / on either side. / What is *not* familiar around us / more relevant / than what is."[32] Here the speaker clearly articulates the guiding paradigm of *(dis)Orient*: to separate the entwinement of the East and West in the European narrative of conquest, to dismantle the imagined land bridge, and to affirm the colonized's or speaker's ability to claim Indigenous knowledge as normative. The speaker questions, "But whose truth, whose meridian / would show your proper placement?"[33] The query points out the colonizer's inability to find a true center or point of orientation that will properly focus a vision of the Indigenous nations and their territories. Ultimately, Stevens uses this method of (dis)Orientation to expose the lack of compass inherent in

European cartography as applied to Native North American and Chinese peoples by the Jesuits and those who arrived thereafter.

Two-Rowed (Two-Spirited) Texts: Mapping the Gaze

The sexualization of conquest and mapped territories is central to the making of meaning in *(dis)Orient* and other poems by Stevens; this technique results in a queering of the gaze and a perforation of supposed lines of separation between colonizer/colonized, European/American/Asian, human bodies and geographic bodies; in fact, this interplay of sameness and difference is critical to Stevens's reading of the Two Row Wampum. Stevens actively queers the Jesuit narrative of conquest and merely recites the always already queer identities of European men living solitary lives *outside* of the heteronormative sanction of marriage, yet *with* the (supposed) heteronormative sanction of monasticism. For instance, the poem's speaker cites the *Relations* directly after reflecting upon "my trips / to the liquid parts of you . . . / the glistening rim of your mouth":

> *Where this great lake discharges its waters, is very*
> *advantageous to perform religious*
> *functions, since it is the great resort of most of the*
> *savages of these regions[.]*[34]

The process of building missions and seeking conversions becomes as much about disciplining the Jesuit body as the Native body into conformity. Maps and desire are conflated as the speaker elaborates upon this affair between Native and European, implying a question of who is being converted: "Last night, my face beneath / the light framework of your knee. / Night anchorage / at Maple bridge / or the matrix of bodily awareness. / Locate me."[35] The invitation to map the speaker's body plays with assumptions about the nature of power between the missionary and the unconverted; in fact, perhaps in the "mapping" of the Native body, the physical encounter transmits knowledges that alter the missionary as much as the unconverted. The liberatory possibilities of a Two Spirit reading in (dis)Orienting and disrupting the colonizer's gaze seem quite potent in this regard. This Two-Spirited mapping is also entwined with Stevens's engagement of the Two Row Wampum wherein the Indigene is located both on the wampum belt and in the physical territory it spatializes.

Stevens continues in a similar vein in the poems that follow *(dis)Orient* proper in *A Bridge Dead in the Water: Three Translations from Characters Found on a Lover's Body, Five Poems from the Paintings of Lang Shining,* and *Remembering Shanghai* collectively extend this process of (dis)Orientation to span the Pacific Ocean and upset Orientalizing processes at play in the colonial and neocolonial eras. As the bridge cannot be forced to function, so must the Two Row be honored for its own affirmation of difference (language, culture) and sameness (sexuality, humanity). The speaker in these poems is unnamed and not overtly racially identified, though as with *(dis)Orient*, the speaker's identity seems likely to be American Indian based on references to the Western Hemispheric Indigenous peoples. Again, a Two Spirit erotic predominates in these poems, as in *Three Translations from Characters Found on a Lover's Body*: "Your mouth is a carriage / and the carriage plus the tenth of a cubit is turn, / bent knuckle revolving around a pivot."[36] Bodies and maps converge again in this series of poems, eliciting different understandings of maps in the process of colonization: "Your torso sings Garden," "the garden of abdomen," and "the horizon of your belly."[37] Stevens plies the tool of (dis)Orientation again here by way of establishing the colonizer's complete lack of center or standard.

Five Poems from the Paintings of Lang Shining take Italian Jesuit painter Giuseppe Castiglione as their subject, and the poems' speaker identifies Lang Shining as "a kind / of brother-in-law."[38] Hence, the writer's role vis-à-vis his subject matter and his position as a man alone in an unknown country makes him a relative by marriage to Lang Shining. Locations are clearly muddied as in earlier poems in the collection: "The half light breeds shadows / beneath the feathered willow. / A half breed lights / on the plain of your chest."[39] This opening observation about location shows the repeated conflation of land and bodies as well as the unlocatable racial other who is always located and locatable in wampum narratives. In fact, in spite of the poems' presumed setting in Lang Shining's China, four out of five poems contain an overt reference to the Western Hemisphere and suggest the speaker's location there: Erie, San Francisco, White Cloud, and "the timetelling plant from the west" are all mentioned. The speaker identifies commonalities in representation across Lang Shining and George Catlin: "Maybe you were right / about the land bridge, / about it all."[40] Finally, the lover's sexual response is likened to a time-telling plant in western North America: "*When touched it goes to sleep, then it wakes. Rare things ought not be praised, but this is strange and deserves a poem.*"[41] Interestingly, the poem's speaker wants to write this quote from the emperor in Chinese ideograms on the lover's body, "as Qianlong scrawled / across the exquisite faces / of paintings."[42] This inscription on the lover's body suggests the need to exert order on Indigenous geographic bodies as illustrated through Stevens's collection of Jesuit narratives of North America and China. Stevens's use of bodies as spaces of colonial desire is antedated in *Tokinish,* and this collection focuses more narrowly on the relationship between conquest, possession, and knowledge through the record of the missionary dictionary. Sarah Dowling describes the conflation of physical bodies and geographic bodies as "a language of colonial metaphors of (sexual) conquest, exploration (of bodies), and possession (of lovers)." She concludes that

> [a]lthough the poem [*Tokinish*] is critical of this proprietary language of desire, it does not seek out a new, nonproprietary language for desire; rather, it gropes its way toward an expression of desire that calls attention to its proprietary character, its way of claiming, and the significance of that claiming. Rather than colonial fantasy, rather than haunting, this is a language of desire that keeps its proprietary function, and the coloniality of that function radically present, always at the forefront. . . . Perhaps what is most surprising about Stevens's text is that it positions queer desire, in the very colonial, very proprietary forms that he describes it, as what encourages the recognition of Native people as fully human subjects. . . . Stevens insists on this language of desire because the way that we unthinkingly use it keeps history active and keeps the colonization of North America and its effects circulating in everyday language.[43]

Dowling's observations regarding *Tokinish* and colonial bodies with their language of property and ownership are in many ways salient and pertinent to Stevens's similar strategies in *(dis)Orient*. Contrastively, Stevens's use of Two Row methodologies in both *Tokinish* and *A Bridge Dead in the Water* challenge the conclusion of subjectivity as elusive in Dowling's framing of *Tokinish*. In fact, the language of colonial propriety inherent in *Tokinish* is contrasted with Indigenous narratives of equality in the Two Row: examples include the Williams dictionary versus wampum records; European maps versus wampum belts and oral traditions. Some maps are based on Native knowledge and seeing, much like reading the wampum.

Two Row Poetics

With regard to *A Bridge Dead in the Water*, Stevens's use of the Two Row methodology predominates in the last two major poems in the collection: *The Mutual Life: Relationships, Colonization, and Other Accidents, A Manual for Reference and Alphabets of Letters, Or A New Primer For The Use of Native or Confused Americans*. What is most significant here is not that Stevens acknowledges the influence that Hodinöhsö:ni' thought has had on his poetry, though earlier collections like *Combing the Snakes from His Hair* and *Tokinish* overtly point out that truth. Instead, through aspects of form, language, and voice, Stevens exercises a new Two Row methodology that is unique to his own voice, and the Two Row methodology seemingly answers the (dis)Orientation of the colonizers' records. In fact, Stevens's Two Row episteme seems directly related to his notion of "running twin rails" of ethnicity and sexuality throughout his poetry.[44]

Based on *The Mutual Life Insurance Company of New York: Accidents, Emergencies, and Illnesses*, which was published in 1901, Stevens's poem *The Mutual Life* is divided into four sections: accidents, fractures, and wounds; emergencies, aches, foreign bodies, and diseases; various poisons; and remedies. Significantly, the remedies section is the shortest. In its original publication, *A Mutual Life* includes illustrations of various treatments in application to the body from the 1901 publication; the aesthetic is vintage, fin-de-siècle. Stevens's decision to illustrate this collection implicates the mnemonic function of wampum in recording oral narratives and alludes to the Two Row specifically. The use of illustrations with print text invokes the streams of Native and European narrative recorded in the wampum as mnemonic aid and spoken word.

At the outset, the poem's title suggests a shared life, perhaps a national one, held in common, and it seems to allude as well to the Iroquois Confederacy that informed much of the structure of the US government with its three branches of government, checks and balances, and union of states. The speaker of *The Mutual Life*, however, is clearly Indigenous and cast out of (or refuses) enfranchisement or membership in this American national collectivity. Further, the form of the insurance plan itself gestures to colonial ironies that explain away the ugliness of land theft and genocide. For instance, the first section of *Accidents*, entitled "Shock," includes smallpox blankets amongst other mishaps; however, the poem's speaker provides instructions for the preparation of these blankets in biological warfare: "Learning / life may be destroyed by certain agencies. . . . Flannels wrung out in hot (pox blankets) / water should not be neglected."[45] The line composition implies the refusal to admit of willful infection of American Indians via smallpox blankets by separating the "agencies" responsible for these "accidents." Further, other ironically labeled "accidents" in the first section of *A Mutual Life* include the following: under "Asphyxia," the mass hanging of 38 Dakota men as retribution for their involvement in the 1862 Dakota Conflict, a protest of the enforced starvation of Dakotas in Minnesota and abrogation of their treaties by the US government via Indian agent Andrew Myrick; under "Dislocations," the relocation of American Indians from reservations in the 1950s and 1960s; and under multiple headings, repeated treatment with brandy as a therapy for injury, alluding to the distribution of alcohol as a means of manipulating American Indians.[46] The classification of these intentional policies as unintentional underscores the poem's subtitle, "Relationships, Colonization, and Other Accidents." Wounds, in fact, are associated with the colonizer's ability to curtail Native storytelling: "Pressure best applied / to the stories, the pulsations / of which can be felt . . . Slip a stick through / the knot twisting / till the story stops flowing."[47] Here the wound of colonization inspires stories, stories that the settler culture would rather see amputated after the use of a tourniquet to staunch the bleeding.

Stevens uses the Two Row by way of re-introducing Native North American narrative into the poem:

Malaria.
Our stories hardened
as veins of flint.   *Kanienkehaka.*

    At first only two   great ones,
    mosquitoes,   one on each side
    of the river,   spearing 5 or many
    warriors   with their large beaks.
    Moving to   other rivers as men
    moved course.   Taking more men,
    pouncing and   devouring hands
    and heads.   20 warriors, 2 canoes
    shoulders slung   with bows. War
    clubs on their belts.   Filled the air
    with many arrows,   half killed in
    their canoes, that   those left could
    fight the creatures on   land, singing
    their death songs   as they went.
    And the creatures   fell to the earth.
    Men tore their   bodies to bits, and
    from their blood   flew millions of
    little mosquitoes,   the air soon full
    with them, angry for   the slaughter
    of their grandfathers.   Hungry for
                        blood.[48]

The poem's speaker here voices two streams of history, embodying the Two Row and its river imagery on the page. The figure of mosquitoes and their subsistence on human blood and spread of malarial disease is noteworthy, insofar as mosquitoes become figures of the cannibalizing and consumptive/consuming nature of European land expropriation and genocide.[49] Significantly, this passage follows the section on "Wounds" that enumerates ways in which to stop the flow of stories. Here, Indigenous stories flow on the page, and they recount the trauma of warfare and the spread of disease. The poem's speaker reflects, "I don't hate you for the death of my grandfathers, though I may blame you now and then for the red bumps in the road, the quinine and the gin."[50] The poem's closing section, "Remedies," suggests that there is no easy cure for the ills of colonization: "I decided last night / to paint you in poisons. . . . Our portrait, a thin red line in a field of white. / The soft palette sore from the remedy." While the colonizer mimics the Two Row in "Mineral Poisons" by listing poisonous paints in two rows on the page, ultimately *A Mutual Life* only provides "indemnity" for "the possible results of both [disease and accident]."[51]

Stevens employs similar Two Row concrete poems in *Tokinish*, such as the following example:

Néepuck.	The blood.
Wunnícheke.	The hand.
Wunnácks.	The bellie.
Mapànnog.	The breast.
Apòme.	The thigh.
Sítchipuck.	The necke.
Wuttòne.	The mouth.
Wuskeésuckquash.	The eyes.
Mscáttuck.	The fore-head.[52]

Regarding passages of this type in *Tokinish*, Dowling concludes "The problem of mutuality in the context of uneven relations of power speaks directly to Stevens's use of the lexical form of the *Key*, where the facing columns of English and Narragansett words appear to be equal, but function very differently."[53] In fact, I would argue that Stevens's columnar form in *Tokinish* is a precursor to his employment of Two Row praxis in *A Bridge Dead in the Water*; thus, while the dictionary entry form showcases attempts at colonial possession through cataloguing Indigenous knowledge, Dowling perhaps overlooks the potency of Narragansett on the page.

Returning to *A Bridge Dead in the Water, Alphabets of Letters, Or A New Primer For The Use of Native or Confused Americans* is an example of the Two Row columns that is notable for its rich infusion of Mohawk language, knowledge, and worldview into its form and aesthetic. In doing so, Stevens strings the Two Row into this poem at a more fundamental level than

A Mutual Life. In the most stunning example of Two Row interpolation from "The Alphabet out of Order," Stevens writes: "It will never be the same. / The alphabet out of order / Your tongue / In mandate direction." The poem continues:

> *Shatikwáthos*   *tsi   nón:we   níhatí:teron.*
> *Tenhsh***theyontátkmeet***en'   iá:ken'   ne*
> *Rona***theyten***ro'shó***friends***n:'a   ne   original*
> **People***nkwehonwé:ke kwáh she's iá:***it is said***ken'* **could**
> **Not***iáh tha'***speak a** *taonta***word***hontá:ti' ne onkw***of the way**
> *Eho***nof the original***wehné***people***ha'.* **Silence.**

The interflowing and interruption of English and Mohawk fracture meaning and provide a visual, phonemic representation of colonization, knowledge, and epistemic splintering. Simultaneously, this dual language use privileges Mohawk in its placement and in its intended audience: few Mohawk readers are completely unable to read English, while many more English readers are unable to read any Mohawk. What begins as a coherent Mohawk narrative is interpolated and interrupted by the English statements, which are a literal translation of a prophecy regarding the arrival of Europeans. Stevens translates the Mohawk passage as follows: "Indian friends will meet, it is said, and they will be unable to speak a single word of Indian."[54] Mohawk is visually shattered on the page by the "mandate direction" of English, leaving the conclusion that the ability of the Original People to speak their own language has been hampered, at best, and lost, at worst, through the mandate of English language education.

The poem's speaker addresses Mohawk chief Joseph Brant who is generally considered a visionary for his negotiation of the Haldimand Treaty, which set aside significant lands for the Six Nations after the Revolutionary War: "Brant, lettered Chief, / you foresaw the missionary meltdown, / understood the alphabet / as more than religious creed. Land. Oil. Gold. Labour."[55] The poem eventually progresses into a far-reaching critique of colonial narrative and economic expropriation of colonized resources that connects mineral rights and land theft in Native North America to the war for oil in Iraq: "*Oi* and *Oy*, are generally hard; as in oil &c. / Let's speak of oil. / The import of brown children to learn / the word / of GOD & OIL. / The indigen as obstacle. You will be removed. . . . 25,000 civilian casualties today, September 2005. The Oi in / oil / is generally hard. / Alaska. Iraq. You will be removed."[56] The speaker asks Brant, "did those little books drag us / from Wheelock's *worse than Egyptian darkness?*"[57] The speaker asserts that Brant "knew" that *"the happiness of the people is constantly sacrificed to the splendour of empire,"* and so also is Brant's relationship to his *"bosom friend,"* Lt. Provost who is "ordered / off to the tropical West Indies." Brant is advised to console himself with another, which he responds to by explaining, "I am Captain John's friend, and a transfer of my affections cannot take place."[58] The poem's own speaker similarly laments the loss of his own love, a French man, who leaves him phone messages in French and Mohawk.

As a way of exerting control over this "alphabet out of order," the speaker refers to "the body / the bravest book" and lists Mohawk vocabulary for the body in two streams of two to four syllables running down the page.[59] Sadly, "even bed bespoke words / can be perfect cheat," and "the rivers of alphabets" beneath the lover's skin lie as well. The speaker addresses Brant again: "lettered Chief, / you saw it in its infancy. / Opened the book / and understood. / **An Alphabet Out of Order.** B R C D G X T L Z N V Y I J M W H K E F A U S O Q P / It would never be the same."[60] The poem closes with this ringing indictment of the duplicity of European agreements in treaties, especially the Two Row, the foundational treaty in which "the rivers of alphabets" agreed to originally have been disordered and altered to fit the needs of the colonizer. That the treachery is both political and sexual fits the larger themes of the entire work and that Brant and the speaker themselves are not able to perform "a transfer of affections" is both a queering of the colonial encounter and a signifier of treaty abrogation in the broadest sense, though located in the specific context of the Two Row in this scenario: the twinning of male lovers and male treaty signatories underscores the meeting of equals that is the basis of the Two Row. Because the colonial narrative is so disordered, at least the versions taught to "Native or Confused Americans," who are confused by virtue of the constant changing of colonial rationales for conquest (i.e., Christianity, liberation from tyranny, salvation from poverty), the reasonable and orderly presentation of Two Row narratives as in "Malaria" draws our attention to this foundational narrative in colonial encounters, one readily put aside by the British and Americans. As the speaker suggests, this treachery was anticipated by Brant who secured a more stable existence for the Six Nations in the Haldimand Treaty, refusing to treat with the Americans who perpetrated the Sullivan-Clinton Campaign.

Regarding the broader pattern of Hodinöhsö:ni' understandings of treaties as agreements made and recorded in wampum, agreements that are understood to be followed in principle, not in letter, Williams and Nelson write:

> Where the written documents vary from the understanding arrived at in the treaty, it must be recalled that those documents themselves are not the treaties. They are merely the record of the treaties, preserved by one side. The full record of the treaties consists of writing, memory, and action. Where there are written records, though, containing technical or legal language, and one party is both unschooled in that law or technology and illiterate, a great deal of caution is required to ascertain that party's understanding of the transaction. The "trust deed" of the 1701 Nanfan Treaty is an excellent example of this kind of problem, for history shows that there were clearly separate understandings, after the fact, of what had been intended.[61]

Other examples of similar misunderstandings or overt exploitation of the *letter* of a given treaty abound, from the Walking Purchase of 1763 to the Sac Treaty of 1802 and beyond. Williams and Nelson are clear that "The Iroquois tradition [of law] is a tradition of responsible thinking" and that the mind is "the medium chosen for recording and recalling the Great Law—and all later important events and decisions."[62] Print records of treaties are only one side's record of what they believe to have transpired, not the actual agreement reached in treaty council. Bringing this awareness of treaty protocol, Hodinöhsö:ni' understandings of the law, and print and wampum records of treaties to our reading of *Alphabets of Letters*, Stevens's design of exposing slippage in language and intent in colonial expressions and deception or deviation from original agreements, such as the Two Row, becomes patently obvious; moreover, Stevens's contributes to and enriches our understanding of how colonial discourses pervade, deceive, and confuse, leaving Indigenous narrative scattered within its (dis)Orienting rationale.

James Stevens's use of the Two Row wampum as an organizing principle and a narrative theoretical mode in *A Bridge Dead in the Water* privileges Indigenous knowledges and encodes them into the poetic genre. Further, in this collection, the Two Row speaks back to colonial "accident" and "(dis)Orientation." Stevens shows the vain strivings of the Jesuits and early explorers to impose an Orientalizing order upon Native North America and Asia, an intellectual failure embodied in the Bering land bridge theory alluded to in the collection's title. The organization of colonial knowledges into an actuarial narrative of mishaps and an alphabet of disheveled letters highlights their failings to account for colonial crimes when contrasted with Indigenous narratives encoded in the Two Row; simultaneously, utilizing a discourse of antiquated encounter, Stevens illustrates the pervasive hold of that language while refusing its totalizing effects with his contemporary Native speaker's vocal response and perspective. What Stevens has accomplished works deeply at the level of epistemology and Indigenous studies: through (dis)Orientation and Two Row narrative, Stevens opens colonial wounds to prepare them for healing. His dramatization of the struggle to read—and have acknowledged—the Two Row illustrates the gap between treaty agreements and the material realities of the contemporary era.

2

The Covenant Chain in Eric Gansworth's Fiction, Poetry, Memoir, and Paintings

*The Canandaigua Treaty Belt as
Critical Indigenous Economic Critique*

The Treaty with the Six Nations of 1794 remains a seminal document in Iroquois-
United States relations. It is also an important part of the history of both peoples,
because it marked a new and inevitable kind of relationship with the emerg-
ing United States and is evidence of one United States road in American Indian
policy. In light of the history of other roads taken, some of which are among
the most tragic and dishonorable in American history, the Canandaigua Treaty
stands as a symbol of what might have been almost as much as it is a symbol of
what came to be.

—John Mohawk (Seneca, Turtle Clan),
"The Canandaigua Treaty in Historical Perspective"[1]

Friendship treaty belts have a long history amongst northeastern
Native Americans. In 1638, the Hurons created a friendship belt to
record their agreement to allow Jesuits to build a wooden church on their
lands. The belt portrays a central cross symbol, flanked on either side by
figures that grasp the cross. The figure immediately to the left is a layper-
son, and the figure immediately on the right is a Wendat.

To the east, there are two Wendats linking hands, and to the west,
there are two Jesuit figures holding hands in friendship with the church
in question woven into the left side of the belt. The significance of this
particular belt with regard to international diplomacy is also weighty: the
Wendat Nation agrees to allow the Jesuits to build their church and not
take up arms against them, provided the Jesuits also pursue a path of
peace. The visual predominance of the landscape in the belt emphasizes

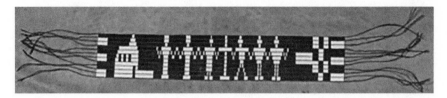

4. Huron Church Belt (1638): reproduction design by Ken Maracle. Photograph by Raymond Skye. Courtesy of Ken Maracle, www.wampumshop.com.

Wendat normativity and political power during this time, and underscores the Wendat Nation's willingness to stand as allies of the Jesuits within their larger social web, to incorporate them, but not to cede territory. The inclusion of the church signifies that the Huron decision to allow the order to build on their lands is noteworthy: the church may be built, but there are no indications of further inroads or favors to be had beyond this agreed-upon measure. The three white horizontal lines flanking the parties at either end of the belt may symbolize equality; however, for the Wendats, these white lines transform into a single white line after transformation via a checkerboard, which may signify change, adverse or otherwise. Finally, the interpolation of figures and white lines confirm the freedom and safety of each group to move through the other's territory.

Other friendship belts include the William Penn Belt, the Treaty of Niagara Belt (1763), the Fort Stanwix Belt (1784), the Great Britain and Six Nations Friendship Belt, the Wolf Belt, the Ojibway and Six Nations Friendship Belt, and many others.[2]

Some of these belts include human figures, while others use abstract shapes (i.e., squares with solid lines connecting them) to indicate the friendship there established. It is also noteworthy that a range of northeastern nations, including Anishinaabeg, Wendat, Lenni Lenape, Azaagi, Wampanoag, Mohegan, Wabenaki, and others, used these belts to affirm friendships, record agreements, and send messages about international affairs (i.e., calls to war, pleas to remain neutral).[3] The original William Penn Belt dates from approximately 1682 or 1683 and features a singular Native figure and European figure holding hands in friendship on a white background. In this belt, size matters: the belt itself is eighteen rows wide, implying the relative importance of the agreement recorded, and

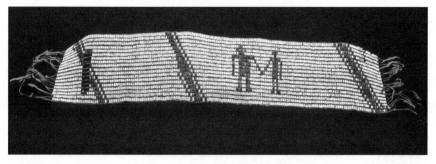

5. William Penn Belt. Courtesy of the Philadelphia History Museum at the Atwater Kent, the Historical Society of Pennsylvania Collection.

the Native figure is physically much larger than the European figure, suggesting the two groups' relative power and significance at the meeting.[4] Long purple chains run diagonally down the left side (one line) and on the right side (two lines), indicating paths through ceded territories where Natives could travel at will without fear of interference.[5]

The friendship belt most often discussed in the contemporary political realm and brought to life through annual commemoration in the United States is the Canandaigua Treaty or Pickering Treaty of 1794.[6] In 1794, over 1,600 Tuscaroras, Senecas, Cayugas, Onondagas, and Oneidas met at "The Chosen Town" or Canandaigua to negotiate and confirm a treaty with Timothy Pickering, a federal agent selected by George Washington.[7] This treaty is often invoked as the foundation for US-Hodinöhsö:ni' relations and with just cause: this treaty was the first comprehensive treaty negotiated after the close of the Revolutionary War, the omission of Native allies in the Treaty of Paris (1783), and the genocidal campaign of generals Sullivan and Clinton into Iroquoia. John Mohawk identifies this treaty as "a seminal document in Iroquois-United States relations," "an important part of the history of both peoples," and "a symbol of what might have been almost as much as . . . a symbol of what came to be."[8] Washington was keen to have Pickering cement the ally status of the Six Nations before beginning a campaign against the Ohio Indians, many of whom were Iroquois, and those tribal nations further west. Senecas were central to this treaty and to securing the necessary protection of a fledgling settler country, given their heavy involvement in the growing intertribal resistance movement, which was organized under the title of United Indian Nations. The Canandaigua Treaty is composed of seven articles: Article One "firmly" establishes "perpetual" "peace and friendship" between the Six Nations and the United States. Article Two acknowledges the presence of reservations belonging to the Six Nations and agrees that "said reservations shall remain theirs, until they choose to sell the same to the people of the United States[.]" Article Three states the exact boundaries of the Seneca reservation lands. Article Four states that each side (United States and Six Nations) acknowledge the boundaries of each other's land and will not disturb the other's people in their enjoyment of the land.[9] Article Five allows for the establishment and use of a road to Buffalo Creek and guarantees Americans "free passage" through Six Nations' lands and "free use of the harbors and rivers adjoining and within their respective tracts of land[.]" Article Six provides for an annual obligation of the US government to provide goods amounting to $10,000 and additional funds "with a view to promote the future welfare of the Six Nations" in perpetuity. Article Seven requires that any injuries or deaths caused by one side to the other will be remedied by official measures, not "private revenge," in order "to preserve our peace and friendship unbroken."[10]

The George Washington Belt itself is composed of non-Native and Indian figures linking hands in friendship with a longhouse in the middle. Visually, the belt affirms that the United States is being brought into the existing peace that is recorded in the Hiawatha Belt, which is itself a representation of a longhouse with a council fire in the middle: Hodinöhsö:ni' political normativity is central to this agreement and was necessary to foreground, in order to secure Hodinöhsö:ni' consensus. Concomitantly, given that Washington commissioned the belt, it is noteworthy that the belt maker surrounded the central smaller Native figures and longhouse with thirteen larger non-Native figures, reflecting a less-than-subtle message about how Washington hoped to define future relationships. An annual commemoration and celebration of this treaty occurs on November 11 in Canandaigua with both US and Hodinöhsö:ni' dignitaries present, and the treaty goods detailed in the treaty, including treaty cloth,

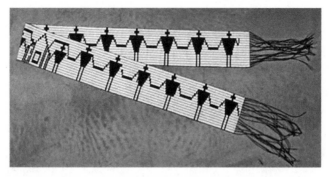

6. Canandaigua Treaty Belt or George Washington Belt (1794): reproduction design by Ken Maracle. Photograph by Raymond Skye. Courtesy of Ken Maracle, www.wampum shop.com.

are also delivered at this time, in affirmation of the agreement originally made in 1794.[11] At present, as various Six Nations governments confront New York State officials over taxation of tobacco and gas on Indian land and casinos, the Canandaigua Treaty sits at the heart of those contentions: the Hodinöhsö:ni' hold tight to the understanding originally arrived at in 1794, and New York State officials are wont to use Six Nations revenues to "solve the current fiscal crisis," as the organization Honor Indian Treaties observes.[12] More recently, under former Seneca Nation of Indians president Robert Odawi Porter, the Seneca Nation laid plans to apply for a US Federal Energy Regulatory Commission license for the Kinzua Dam in fall 2013.[13] The argument for Seneca primacy in the competition for this license against the incumbent FirstEnergy, a for-profit utility company, is the language of the Canandaigua Treaty, which specifically mentions free use of the river waters, which by extension include those waters passing through the Kinzua hydroelectric dam. Moreover, given that the Kinzua Dam runs over the Cornplanter Grant, which was flooded by the dam's creation in the 1960s, the Seneca Nation of Indians' right to operate the dam originates directly in treaty rights. Current Seneca Nation president Barry E. Snyder Sr. states, "We are presently considering what remedies to seek for FirstEnergy's past and current unauthorized use of our lands and any potential environmental harm it has caused[:] fixing a wrong and taking back what rightfully belongs to the Seneca Nation."[14] Thus, the Canandaigua Treaty is a living narrative and agreement in Seneca memory, community, and international politics; the Canandaigua Treaty, with its concomitant conditions and terms, participates as a living entity and agent in an ongoing process of Indigenous-settler alliance and diplomacy within the Seneca national imaginary.

This essay explores how Onondaga author and artist Eric Gansworth weaves images of the Canandaigua Treaty Belt and other friendship belts into paintings included in numerous fictional and poetic works, especially *A Half-Life of Cardiopulmonary Function* and *Smoke Dancing*. Gansworth both comments upon the agreement recorded in the Canandaigua Treaty Belt and innovates the visual code of the friendship belt and, specifically, the Canandaigua Treaty Belt in his print narratives. In *A Half-Life of Cardiopulmonary Function*, for instance, Gansworth invokes the visual code of wampum figures as part of a covenant chain that spans the physical and the spirit worlds; simultaneously, these figures, whether rendered in wampum, in a naturalistic style, or in cornhusks, are inscribed with multiple meanings (political, aesthetic, gendered, etc.) that extend the significatory reach of wampum from the historical realm to the politically prescient to the emotionally empowering. Meanwhile, in *Smoke Dancing*, Gansworth explores the rights vouchsafed in the Canandaigua Treaty and their applications or expressions in contemporary contexts (i.e., "those stories . . . keep playing themselves out to this very day"), while bringing the economics of this friendship belt to the visual conversation between paintings in the novel.[15] Finally, *Rabbit Dance*, a play, stages the gains to be made in equal exchange between Native and non-Native women's traditions and affirms the treaty rights enacted by Tuscarora women who vend beadwork at Niagara Falls as part of the Porter Agreement. In all three of these works, Gansworth figuratively "turns the belt" to communicate that the relationships affirmed in the Canandaigua Treaty Belt are in disorder, and he engages the poverty narrative, as defined by Roxanne Rimstead, and the trope of laboring hands within the friendship chain as strategies in an Indigenous economic critique.

In the larger body of his poetry, fiction, drama, and paintings, Gansworth develops a unique Hodinöhsö:ni' visual code that includes wampum and beadwork as distinct representational strategies and intellectual traditions; this essay will focus on the role of the friendship belt particularly, while acknowledging these larger investments in Iroquois intellectual practices and visual iconography and their relationships to contemporary economic realities in Iroquoia. In "Embodying Life in Art," Christopher Teuton makes the following observation about wampum in Gansworth's work: "Wampum, the carved quahog shells first introduced to the Haudenosaunee people by Hiawatha, serve as Gansworth's symbol of communication and connection. . . . Unlike alphabetic writing, wampum belts do not reproduce speech, rather they signal a different set of communicative values rooted in community. For the message of a wampum belt to continue, that message must be remembered in a living, human community."[16]

In this essay, I pick up on Christopher Teuton's observation about the function and necessity of memory in wampum's performance, and I argue that we remember in a very localized way, thinking of the Canandaigua Treaty Belt and its specific relationship to the Tuscarora Nation and the larger Confederacy in Gansworth's work. Moreover, I maintain that readers must consider the implications of a Canandaigua Treaty-based ethos in Gansworth's fiction and poems as necessarily addressing pragmatically oriented concerns that are outlined in the treaty itself. To that end, I connect an Indigenous economic critique based in wampum records to a body of working-class studies scholarship by Roxanne Rimstead and Janet Zandy via which I read the hands of the friendship chain as signs of a surplus laboring hand: this hand mirrors and exceeds the laboring hand as depicted in Zandy's study, *Hands*, and I read these hands as markers of consensus and agreement within a woodlands economic, political, and spiritual social fabric.

Hands in friendship chains tie Natives and non-Natives together in the geospatial economic fabric of Native North America. For instance, the Canandaigua Treaty Belt ties settlers into the longhouse confederacy, and these hands, thus, link non-Natives in the ceremonial, political, and economic understandings implicit in longhouse protocols and wampum teachings. The hands' figurative placement on a background of white signifies non-Native agreement to enter and maintain the Great Law of Peace. In *Hands: Physical Labor, Class, and Cultural Work*, Janet Zandy approaches the subject of hands and working-class identity, claiming hands as "maps to history and culture" and "aids to retrieving or associating ideas."[17] In Zandy's study, hands are tied intrinsically to the mind and the knowledge carried therein; much like Indigenous epistemological practices, she refuses Cartesian duality of mind/body splits. Zandy writes:

> This book . . . moves toward cultural retrieval and reclamation. . . . Out of loss emerge cultural responses, recoveries, remembrances, and articulations. . . . In linking forms of cultural expression with physical labor, *Hands* centers what is usually decentered—variegated, unstable, and complex culture of workers. . . . [L]aboring bodies harbor an epistemology, a way of knowing and understanding the world that comes out of the physicality of work.[18]

Zandy's class-based analysis with its focus upon the knowledge carried in hands provides one avenue for reading friendship chains in treaty belts as economic agreement and their invocation by storytellers, like Gansworth, as economic critique.

Gansworth's depictions of poverty also speak to a larger discourse surrounding poverty narratives and their analysis, which scholars like Roxanne Rimstead and Sean Teuton have engaged extensively. Rimstead claims the term "poverty narrative" as "a category that includes stories both by and about the poor;" further, she acknowledges that "no one overarching theory of poverty can make all poverty narratives coherent."[19] Reflecting on Native American poverty and literary critical studies, Sean Teuton contends, "Any portrait of modern American Indian life that seeks cultural objectivity thus cannot avoid an account of Indian poverty." Teuton criticizes Sherman Alexie's depiction of poverty in *Reservation Blues* as "risk[ing] playing into the hands of mainstream readers who wish to believe Native people are socially degenerate."[20] Contrastively, Teuton succinctly argues, "poverty can and should be externalized as a colonial imposition—not internalized as evidence of Indian inferiority."[21] Teuton finds a successful example of a decolonizing critique of federal policy as impoverishing American Indians in Betty Louise Bell's *Faces in the Moon*: "*Faces in the Moon* invites readers to consider the sources and consequences of Indian poverty, and it offers, if not a solution, then at least a resolution, through a process of remembering and healing that all of us can understand."[22] Throughout his work that depicts or otherwise addresses the Canandaigua Treaty Belt and treaty-related concerns, Eric Gansworth also accessibly portrays Hodinöhsö:ni' poverty and its origins and trajectory from treaty to reservation and beyond.[23] While acknowledging the grim realities that follow from treaty violations, Gansworth illustrates American Indian resilience and determination and showcases the "unnatural" aspects of Hodinöhsö:ni' poverty.[24] Ultimately, his use of the treaty in performing this incisive economic critique contributes significantly to our understanding of Iroquois intellectual traditions and transmission; moreover, Gansworth successfully "extends the rafters" of the longhouse to apply these knowledges in contemporary settings.

Eric Gansworth is an Onondaga (Eel Clan) who was born and raised on the Tuscarora Reservation near Lewiston, New York. His family's history reaches back into the incorporation of the Tuscarora into the Five Nations in 1722, when several Onondaga clanmothers accompanied the Tuscaroras to the Niagara region where Senecas shared their traditional territories to include their southern Iroquois relatives subsequent to their adoption.[25] Gansworth's family is descended from these eighteenth-century clanmothers. Gansworth attended the Tuscarora Indian School, learning Tuscarora language in school and at home, and he later attended Niagara County Community College where he earned an AA in Electroencephalography, a choice he made based on his own family's value for hospital work.[26] During these studies, he continued writing horror stories, an endeavor he began at age fourteen, and shortly afterwards, he met his literary mentor and completed his first book-length work, a horror novel. Later, seeking credibility for his burgeoning body of fiction and poetry, Gansworth earned a BA and MA in English at the State University College at Buffalo where he completed a master's thesis on virus tropes in William S. Burroughs' fiction. While teaching as an adjunct, Gansworth worked to complete a second horror novel when "out of nowhere, 'The Ballad of Plastic Fred' came out one day instead of the next horror chapter. A few days later, 'Gazebos.' To this day, I have no idea what happened."[27] After attending the first Returning the Gift Conference of Native American Writers in 1992, Gansworth felt he had found a direction for the fiction he had been writing; while no immediate publications came from attending this conference, Gansworth was introduced to a network of American Indian authors that he would progressively become a part of over the ensuing years.[28] In 1993 he completed the first draft of *Indian Summers*, which he placed for publication in 1998.[29] The years that followed saw the publication of a growing body of work. His fictional works include *Indian Summers* (1998), *Smoke Dancing* (2004), *Mending Skins* (2005), *Extra Indians* (2010), and *If I Ever Get Out of Here* (2013); his poetry collections are *Nickel Eclipse: Iroquois Moon* (2000) and *A Half-Life of Cardiopulmonary Function* (2008); he also published one mixed-genre collection, *Breathing the Monster Alive* (2006). Moving onto the stage in recent years, Gansworth has had four plays staged: *Re-Creation Story* (2008), *Home Fires and Reservation Roads* (2011), *Patriot Act* (2011), and *Rabbit Dance* (2011). The uniting thread that is woven throughout all of these works is Gansworth's visual code, and to underscore this point, his paintings appear in all but *Rabbit Dance*, which overtly addresses beadwork traditions in its plot.[30] The paintings themselves portray Hodinöhsö:ni' characters in contemporary settings and are informed by an aesthetic that grows from Iroquois iconography and cultural traditions (i.e., wampum, beadwork, social dances, oral tradition). Gansworth describes this technique as "a commentary on the oral tradition existing within Haudenosaunee culture and its fluid nature" that "uses iconography recognizable in the context of the mythic Haudenosaunee world, yet alters it to reflect issues relevant to a more contemporary Haudenosaunee existence."[31] Gansworth currently is Professor of English at Canisius College, and he has held residencies at Michigan State University, Associated Colleges of the Twin Cities, the Seaside Institute, the Institute of American Indian Arts, State University of New York - Oneonta, and Ohio Northern University. *Mending Skins* won the PEN Oakland-Josephine Miles National Literary Award in 2006 and was selected for Picturing America Series for Public Libraries in 2010; other work by Gansworth has been nominated for the Pushcart Prize (2006) and selected for the National Book Critics Circle's "Good Reads" List (2008), as well as College Libraries' America Reads (2000). Most recently, *Extra Indians* (2011) won the American Book Award.

Friendship Chains, Condolence, and *A Half-Life of Cardiopulmonary Function*

In *A Half-Life of Cardiopulmonary Function*, Gansworth retells the story of his older brother's untimely death in 2000 in paintings and poetry. As Gansworth notes in the foreword to the book:

> I continued to work largely, as I had for a number of years, almost exclusively in purple and white, the colors of wampum, the beads used to create belts that held all of Haudenosaunee cultural ideas. I had been inspired by Laurie Anderson's discussion of "Zero and One" in her film, *Home of the Brave*, and in homage to the understanding of wampum that she gave me through this monologue, I began calling this body of visual work "Indigenous Binary Code." I wanted to take the idea further by including images borrowed from popular culture, medical texts, family members who were willing to be models, friends, traditional imagery, formal western representation, objects from my home, all in communication with one another, creating hybrid new narratives by illuminating the old ones with different light sources.[32]

A Half-life of Cardiopulmonary Function represents a deepening in Gansworth's approach to wampum imagery in his novels and poetry; by overtly moving toward operating wholly in "the Haudenosaunee binary code," Gansworth makes a claim for the Hodinöhsö:ni' tradition as "a thinking tradition," as Williams and Nelson term it, and self-consciously extends the purview of *Ga'nigöi:yoh* ("the Good Mind").[33] In explaining the significance of the Good Mind, Nicholle Dragone writes: "The Good Mind, as an element of Haudenosaunee thought, a basic tenet of Haudenosaunee culture, and as a tool to discipline the mind, is peace, health, and reason. It is caring, co-existence, fairness, integrity, respect, and reasoning."[34] To that end, in this collection Gansworth invites us into the Good Mind, in order to consider "the ongoing relevance of wampum as both the medium and the message of sovereignty," as Susan Bernardin articulates it.[35] Further, Bernardin reads wampum strings in the "Cross-Pollination" image from *A Half-Life of Cardiopulmonary Function* "as portals to resilient memory and creative adaptation"; in turn, this portion of the essay will pursue such a reading of wampum throughout this collection.[36]

A Half-Life of Cardiopulmonary Function depicts the numerous ways that lives can be divided or fractionated: there is the half-life of decomposing radioactive (or otherwise toxic) material; the double life of an individual who feels a tension between his or her community and his or her individual path; the lives cut short of both John Lennon and Gansworth's brother. Similarly, this poetry collection also focuses upon a leitmotif of loss, the loss of loved ones through death, divorce, or other parting, and the role of those who mourn or continue to "Imagine," as Gansworth dubs it in an allusion to Lennon's oeuvre.

Gansworth repeats the friendship chain throughout the collection visually and narratively; male wampum figures, naturalistically drawn men, and cornhusk dolls recur in differing settings, while allusions to treaty rights as vested in the Canandaigua Treaty are affirmed through these images and also directly alluded to in subject matter, such as "Where the Dawes Act Finds Its Voice Even Now in Northern New York." This collection possesses many layers and their interrelated complexity is sometimes dizzying to capture; Gansworth writes of *A Half-Life* in the drafting stage, when the collection possessed three separate narrative threads:

> For a while, I believed I was working on two separate books, *CrossPolliNation* and *A Half-Life of Cardio-Pulmonary Function*. The first continued my earlier explorations—the ways in which contemporary indigenous peoples navigate a long-standing traditional culture and at the same time embrace popular culture. The second focused on enduring the difficulties in our lives and grew from, among other things, the sudden and unexpected death of my oldest brother in 2000. . . .
>
> It became clear, a couple incarnations ago, that a third book was emerging. It started as one poem in what I considered the "pop culture" section of *Cross-PolliNation*, a small piece about a terrible Bigfoot movie I

love, *The Legend of Boggy Creek*. Once the poem was done, though, more came, and soon there were too many not to warrant an explicit place of their own.[37]

Even with the Bigfoot section of the collection removed, *A Half-Life* explores manifold permutations of the topics in question, navigations of traditional and popular cultures and survival of a given life's difficulties; simultaneously, Gansworth's compositional process of *A Half-Life* represents a literary process modeled on longhouse councils in which two sides of the fire pass an idea back and forth while a third makes the ultimate decision.[38] While the Bigfoot section of the collection has departed and fashioned a separate existence as *Breathing the Monster Alive*, another poetry collection by Gansworth, the remnants of its decisive role remain in the numerous references to and solidifying narrative presence of popular culture as manifested in Pink Floyd and the Beatles. Not simply objects of a materially-driven contemporary popular culture, the music of these bands provide narrative structure and guiding voices to *A Half-Life of Cardiopulmonary Function*, as seen in events like the speaker's visits to the Dakota building where Lennon was shot and the neighboring Strawberry Fields.[39]

Friendship chains connect numerous narrative threads across this collection: they connect wampum and naturalistically drawn men embracing across time, space, and death; they connect individuals together through cornhusk dolls and the people they represent in a parallel figuration to wampum friendship chains; they signify as the Canandaigua Treaty Belt itself and other friendship belts; and, finally, friendship chains provide a political and economic critique of the larger American settler society. In *Inspiration*, the theme of two brothers separated by death is communicated in the Iroquois iconography of two wampum figures, white and purple, that are being released in clouds of tobacco smoke: the differing figures may signify the separation of the two brothers across death (white = death and transcendence of the physical plane, purple = life and mourning), or they may signify the split between spirit and physical body that happens at the moment of death, "the traditional Haudenosaunee path of souls . . . who leave the earth, go under water, and then shoot up into the sky like fiery comets," as Neal Keating observes.[40] Regardless of the interpretation, the figures weave in the sky, interlocked in Gansworth's concept of CrossPolliNation: "creating hybrid new narratives by illuminating old ones with different light sources."[41]

Two larger composite drawings that begin the sections entitled "Beat: Where the Dawes Act Finds Its Voice" and "Pause: The Rain, the Rez, and Other Things" include depictions of a normal EKG wave connecting a purple and a white wampum figure in a friendship chain, and of Gansworth (purple wampum figure) mourning his brother's interment (white wampum figure) in the earth as rain falls with no friendship chains connecting them.

Using naturalistically drawn men on a background of friendship chains, Gansworth thematically connects the mid-section of the collection to the initial painting, "Inspiration"; here we see the brother in death with his eyes cast down and Gansworth in mourning beside the tobacco plants of the earlier painting. In a second naturalistically drawn piece, the men are now standing with the brother centrally located, holding hands with a hand on each side in the friendship chain, though we do not see Gansworth's face, nor do we see the brother's face as it is obscured by the seam of the book. This image seemingly suggests a continued existence of the brother in the covenant chain, though his individual identity may be temporarily vanquished by death (i.e., "raising up" of dead *hoyane:h*); simultaneously, both images imply a possible double life, and in the second painting, that double life lies unacknowledged at the margins of the painting. The overarching implication and cumulative effect of these paintings gesture toward wampum's origin in comforting individuals in mourning, as they originally soothed Ha:yëwënta' as he mourned the loss of his wife and three daughters. In Paul Wallace's retelling of wampum's creation, Ha:yëwënta' says, "This would I do if I found anyone burdened with grief even as I am. I would take these shell strings in my hand and console them. The strings would become words and lift away the darkness with which they are covered. Holding these in my hand, my words would be true."[42] Not only do wampum strings provide comfort, the beads are literally transformed into the words of condolence.

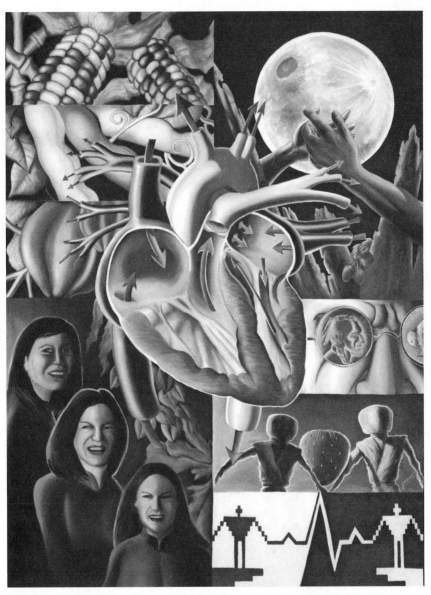

7. Eric Gansworth, "Beat I: Where the Dawes Act Finds Its Voice," from *A Half-Life of Cardiopulmonary Function*. Image © Eric Gansworth, used with permission.

8. Eric Gansworth, "Pause I: The Rain, the Rez, and Other Things," from *A Half-Life of Cardiopulmonary Function*. Image © Eric Gansworth, used with permission.

Gansworth follows these images of realistically drawn men and their wampum figure doubles with a pair of cornhusk dolls, one portrayed in reasonable light and the other in growing shadows; the allusion here to both life and death (light and dark) and the balancing relationship between the twins, Sapling and Flint, seems clear. For the reader of *A Half-Life of Cardiopulmonary Function*, these images are a reminder that death is necessary for life and vice versa, and that mourners must guard against being overwhelmed by grief to the point that it threatens the Good Mind. Similarly, the paired cornhusk dolls allude to the human and wampum friendship chains that unite the brothers across distance and death. Gansworth goes so far as to include instructions for how to make cornhusk dolls in the collection, and this inclusion overtly alludes to the oral tradition that cornhusk dolls were used by men on long hunting trips to remind them of their distant loved ones.[43] In this innovation, the cornhusk doll can be used as a reminder of a loved one after death, while photographs that the family sends back and forth to Vietnam during his brother's tour in the army serve as talismans or guarantees of the continuance of the brother and the family. Photos serve as a friendship chain that ties Hodinöhsö:ni' individuals across time and distance in both *A Half-Life* and other works by Gansworth like *Smoke Dancing*.[44] Gansworth ties cornhusk dolls to the IMAGINE (Gansworth's capitalization) theme in "Beat I: Learning to Speak," which portrays figures from the cover of *Meet the Beatles* as cornhusk dolls in a nine-piece composite painting that features the engraving from the monument in Strawberry Field.[45]

Friendship chains possess a guiding epistemic function in *A Half-Life of Cardiopulmonary Function* as Gansworth uses the implied presence and prevailing truths of the Canandaigua Treaty to enact a political and economic critique of the larger American society. While Gansworth overtly invokes the Canandaigua Treaty Belt visually, he also similarly alludes to the Treaty in numerous references to treaty cloth, borders, and the raw poverty of his upbringing (a product of economic collapse at Tuscarora resulting from the United States not honoring the Canandaigua Treaty). The collection's title poem articulates its assessment of the poverty of reservation life and its implied critique of the larger economic forces of settler society that ensure the wealth of the "truly" American:

I used to think
that if I loved hard
enough and long enough
passion would always win out

like the way I loved
cologne, venturing teenaged into
congested malls, abusing testers
only a salesperson surly enough

inquiring if he or she could help
me in any way, spitting
the prices of even the smallest
bottles of the scents I had

slathered on, forcing me out
in a cloud of confidence
that I was the Calvin Klein
Man, not the Old Spice

Man, not the Zest
Man, and certainly not
the My Drafty House Is Warmed Badly
by Kerosene Heaters Man

impervious to my real
life where I would sneak
down in the middle
of the night, passing

snow collecting
on the inside of the window
sill, trying to descend
the stairs silently

to complete the night lying
before the stove's vents blowing

sooty, warm air deep into my
sleeping lungs, clutching

a broken lacrosse stick
to intimidate rats so brazen
our housecats accepted
them as equal occupants. . . . [46]

The speaker's reverie continues as he recounts the contrasted wealth of the white mall patrons who have "cigarette packs' worth / of what they call spare / change" and "chlorinated well water." Their possession of surplus cigarette money implicates the larger economic relationship between tobacco trade at Tuscarora and the non-Native world's buying power, laying bare the economic relationships that Sean Teuton highlights as fundamental to responsible Native American literary production.[47] The kerosene heaters of the speaker's youth are markers of the impoverishment at Tuscarora and the concomitant danger they pose with their "sooty, warm air" and their tendency to cause rashes of house fires, such as the one suffered by Gansworth's mother.[48] The border between mall and reservation is clearly demarcated as the speaker returns home and is embraced by his sister-in-law who "loves / the scent of burned heating / oil on men," and the mention of the reservation's border also directly alludes to the Canandaigua Treaty and treaties in general.[49] Further, the time period of this enduring poverty is both left in the past and yet constantly present for the speaker: while snow settles "on the proper side of the pane" in his sister-in-law's house, the speaker holds his breath, waiting for the return of his friend, a kind of emotional poverty.

The hardships portrayed by Gansworth are both economic and emotional, as shown in the lines of "Everyone Had a Hard Year," a reflection on his family's failure to gather on the one year memorial of his brother's death.[50] Thus, the treaty-based critique of reservation poverty that Gansworth undertakes consistently acknowledges the economic toll that poverty borne of treaty devaluation creates. The house fires and rat infestations that perform toccata and fugue in Gansworth's poetic memoir do not arise in a vacuum. In fact, Gansworth delineates the origins of this poverty, in the loss of land and in the struggle to enforce treaties, with the clarity Sean Teuton proposes in *Red Land, Red Power.* The recurring image of (treaty) cloth directs the reader's mind to the Canandaigua Treaty throughout the collection. In "Where the Dawes Act Finds Its Voice Even Now in Northern New York," Gansworth directly refers to the treaty cloth used by a young Mohawk named Stan who makes him a water drum with it; meanwhile, the poet reflects on the drum at home, lamenting that "the art of stretching a water drum . . . was lost to me two generations ago" when his grandparents were sent to Carlisle Indian School.[51] Gansworth's sense of cultural loss ("whatever voice / trees speaking to young / Mohawk men use") is muted by his acknowledgement of his own imbrication in popular culture post-Carlisle, alluding to the deer hide being "stretched / across that hollow universe" in homage to the Beatles, and simultaneously noting the Dawes Act as a forced imposition upon the Tuscarora Nation, their treaties, and himself by extension.[52] There is a scarcity of access to traditional knowledges that is embodied in the small shred of treaty cloth that holds the water drum taut and which Gansworth agonizes over losing. Further developing the leitmotif of this cloth, the speaker shops in "Century Twenty-One" post-9/11 and finds "new clothes / remind me of Septembers and the one chance I had / every year to make an impression we could afford / a whole new set of clothes instead of one shirt."[53] These lines include layered meanings that encompass the Canandaigua Treaty and promise of treaty cloth, the economic crippling at Tuscarora after the New York State seizure of their lands for the reservoir, and the complete economic reduction of a Tuscarora who still remains a "shirt wearer."[54] Despite epidemic poverty, the Tuscaroras built a booming economy out of their individual allotments in the early twentieth century, and even after those lands were stolen and put under water, Gansworth illustrates Tuscarora ingenuity in crafting cornhusk dolls as illustrative of "the ways one makes something / out of nothing."[55] In fact, in "Learning to Speak," the speaker entreats the listener to "remember the husk is not a useless part of the body": in this economy even seemingly useless products of growth can be repurposed to perform a meaningful function.[56]

The border of the reservation, as invoked in the Canandaigua Treaty, is further alluded to in the text. Compellingly, this border is often rigid and untraversable, a signifier of the turned Canandaigua Treaty Belt, which expressly provided for the ability to travel freely through Six Nations' territories. For instance, when Gansworth returns to his family's old, now-charred house to retrieve blackcap (berry) plants, the plants fiercely cling to the soil and refuse to leave ("would not give / up thorny trunks nor imbedded / fingers holding fast to earth"); later the speaker reminds himself that "reservation wild berries almost never cross the border."[57] In "(Not) Born in the USA," Gansworth portrays an impending parting of ways with a friend, a separation symbolized by their differing feelings for Bruce Springsteen and their origins on different sides of the Tuscarora-US border. The implicit critique of capital is clear in Gansworth's chafing at Springsteen's "nickname harboring / such negative connotations," his dancing with Courtney Cox "as if at some corporate / Christmas party," and the speaker's friend's assurance that Springsteen "gives good [Halloween] treats," though he does not hand them out himself.[58] Springsteen's imposition of hierarchy in distributing candy to trick-or-treaters flies directly in the face of a Hodinöhsö:ni' sensibility, as depicted by Gansworth in New Year's celebrations and feasts throughout his body of work.[59] Gansworth closes the poem with a depiction of the great divide of nationality that separates the speaker from his friend:

9
The reservation does not allow
for the directions our lives have taken
denies people the fabrication
that relationships never existed
having so much history already
rewritten on us, we accept things
happen and that we will collect
scars from each other over time.
10
In trying to rebuild the bridge
between you and me, the United States
and the reservation, I ask you to the return
concert at the end of the tour, but you list

all the reasons we cannot go, except the real one
that America never forgives indiscretions
except those within its own borders.[60]

This insistence upon the prior existence of relationships directly references treaties, and, in the case of Gansworth's collection, the Canandaigua Treaty with its friendship chain and insistence upon borders between
tribal nation and settler nation stands central to this observation. In spite
of having "so much history already / rewritten on us," the memory of
original nation-to-nation agreements prevails, and the speaker's non-
Native friend's and the United States' refusal to "forgive[] indiscretions
/ except those within its own borders" overtly refers to continued racism and a kind of willful erasure of Indigenous presence. This denial of
contiguity between the United States and the Tuscarora Nation is also
affirmed by the speaker's high school friend who now lives in NYC: "he
shakes his head / at my density, my lack of understanding that my home
and his / are, these days, mutually exclusive environments."[61] Despite the
disavowal of Indigenous knowledge and narrative reflected in these attitudes, the speaker observes a phenomenal, fiery sunset and affirms that
"only the reservation would allow me / the opportunity to view it."[62] Only
situated from Indigenous territory is one able to fully apprehend reality
and the beautiful cyclical finality of sunset.

Friendship Chains, Hands, and Labor in *Smoke Dancing*

Gansworth first engages the Canandaigua Treaty Belt in a sustained print
narrative in his 2004 novel, *Smoke Dancing*, which treats the controversy
around smoke shops on Iroquois reservations and reserves. In this novel,
Gansworth articulates the Canandaigua Treaty Belt as a critique of federal Indian policy and metaphorically invokes a longstanding tradition
of dishonored friendship belts (i.e., Niagara Treaty Belt). The voices of Fiction Tunny, Bud Tunny, Patricia Tunny, Mason Rollins, Big Red Harmony,
Two-Step Harmony, and Ruby Pem narrate the contemporary challenges
surrounding applications of the Canandaigua Treaty to the tobacco trade
and the missteps of clanmothers and chiefs in an era of increasing Christianization and corruption. The novel also succinctly articulates both

the struggles against outside cultural forces (i.e., Christianity, capitalism) and against grinding poverty as what Sean Teuton terms "colonial
imposition[s]." Neither streams of cultural hegemony are naturalized in
the poverty narrative of *Smoke Dancing*; their origins and intended effects
are sketched in concise detail, allowing no misattribution of the causes
of these Indigenous struggles and suffering to Tuscarora actors, while
the complexity of individual characters' social rank and its relationship
to their relative status and matrilineal descent progressively adds depth
to this portrayal.[63] The novel on the whole develops a leitmotif of "survival money," which is made on last-second beadwork sales, fundraisers,
yard sales, and change spirited out of worn clothes and dresser drawers.[64]
Finally, the novel offers differing paradigms of Indigenous labor relations
through businesses run by Bud Tunny and Mason Rollins, respectively,
and the Canandaigua Treaty Belt teachings are central to the standard
articulated by Gansworth therein.

The novel begins with a prologue entitled "Women's Shuffle" and is
divided into three major sections that are each named for Iroquois social
dances: Rabbit Dance, Standing Quiver Dance, and Smoke Dance. Three
is a significant number in Iroquois culture generally and also has specific
applications to the structure and function of Hodinöhsö:ni' political process (i.e., issues are "deposited" in the well of one clan, while proposals are
suggested by a second clan and then "passed over the fire" to a third side
that makes the final decision).[65] In this way, consensus is arrived at, and
agreements (i.e., wampum law) are made. This tripartite allusion underscores the novel's focus upon treaty rights, traditional chiefs and clanmothers, and their involvement or withdrawal from corrupt proceedings
like the flooding of Tuscarora lands in 1960. Some of the pivotal betrayals
that occur in the novel are Ruby Pem's selection of Bud Tunny for a traditional chief, despite her knowledge that he has left the traditional way of
life in childhood; the benefit of particular chiefs and their social circle from
the building of the reservoir and the losses of those who are not politically
aligned with powerful figures; subsequent land swindles engineered by
Bud Tunny in the name of the Tuscarora Nation; Bud Tunny's withholding
acknowledgement of Fiction Tunny as his daughter conceived outside of
his marriage to Twila Tunny; Bud Tunny and other chiefs' refusal to take

action regarding poor water quality, which results in the death of several people including Ruby Pem, Tunny's clanmother.

The plot of the novel follows the rising conflict between Bud Tunny and Mason Rollins, a smoke shop entrepreneur, over the legality of Rollins' business, which Tunny and, by extension, the Tuscarora Nation refuse to sanction, though Rollins claims he is merely acting on Canandaigua Treaty rights that individuals like Bud have profited from for years.[66] Gansworth's depiction of Tunny's apple and cider business and Rollins' tobacco and gasoline venture illustrates important differences in the exercise of treaty rights for individual or group profit. For example, for many years, Bud Tunny is the only individual to benefit from Tuscarora tax-free status through his apple orchard, which he operates using child labor paid at below minimum wage in inhumane working conditions; children are penalized for going inside to take a break as they pick apples, which will be sold off-reservation to businesses that will vend the product as alcoholic cider.[67] The only party to benefit beyond "survival money" from this endeavor will be Tunny and his family who enjoy a large, well-furnished house at the top of the dyke where they have the best possible view of the Niagara River without being included in the flooded post-reservoir lands.[68] In contrast, Rollins comes into his apprehension of treaty rights secured in the Treaty of Canandaigua through the education he receives from Bertha Monterney, who adopts him as one of her dance group. After a struggle with drinking, Rollins decides he wants something better for himself, and while his initial motivation for creating his tobacco and gasoline business is individual profit, he both creates a business that protects workers' rights *and* also makes the workers, other Tuscaroras and unrecognized tribal members, into shareholders in Smoke Rings. In contrast to Tunny's insistence that young children suffer wage reduction if they could not bear the cold and needed to go inside, Rollins equips all of his gas station workers with high quality space age snowsuits that protect them from the cold as they work outside.[69] There are numerous other telling differences in their business practices, including Mason's creation of a Tribal Recreation Building and health insurance that serves all Indians living on-reservation, not just enrolled Tuscaroras; however, most importantly, Gansworth's portrait illustrates that while readers may sympathize with Tunny's espousal of "traditional" ideals, Rollins remakes values of consensus, kinship, and the common pot in his seemingly opportunistic business venture. While Rollins is a visionary in his reclamation of the Onguiaahra Nation, a gesture to the multitribal era in the Niagara region and the Neutral Nation that inhabited the peninsula, Gansworth occasionally provides glimpses of a non-capitalistic economy based on exchange, which is potentially the only secure path to obviating the damage to the land caused by storing industrial waste (i.e., Ezekiel Tunny) or selling gasoline (i.e., Mason Rollins). Big Red Harmony reflects on Mason's liberation economy: "Folks don't like to be given things. Their loyalty is better gained by some kind of cooperation. . . . [T]he exchange system worked."[70]

The novel is visually encapsulated in its cover and title page images, which comment upon the growing complications of relationships between tradition, treaties, and innovation, while the images that accompany the novel's three sections trace Fiction's navigation of these challenges. Gansworth avoids being prescriptive in his conclusions, choosing instead to portray this complexity from an array of vantage points in both visual and print narratives. In the novel's cover image, "The Three Sisters (I): Embrace," corn, beans, and squash are entwined with gasoline hoses and the Canandaigua Treaty Belt, which follow the path of the beans up the stalks of the corn and benefit from the coverage provided by the squash plant's leaves.

Significantly, this placement results in the belt being "turned," signifying to the viewer that the agreement is not being honored. In the novel's prologue, Fiction comments directly upon this image:

> Those three sisters of ours, they're supposed to sustain the rest of us, but also one another. . . . They each have to bring something different . . . from different families. And what is it the beans bring? Nitrogen, one of the key elements of TNT; and if you listen, you'll hear the potential in the explosive laughter of those Indian women. And those Indian men, they want to get closer and back away at the same time—they want to know who the women are laughing at, but they are just as afraid it might be them. And some men don't even want to even take the chance, don't want the women

9. Eric Gansworth, "The Three Sisters (I): Embrace," from *Smoke Dancing*. Image © Eric Gansworth, used with permission.

to come together; but we are survivors, and sometimes the stories unfold themselves slowly before your very eyes, so slowly you don't even know you're one of the players until you see your fingers reaching up, tender shoots wrapping around someone sturdier, steadying yourself on their strength. . . . The storms around us are deadlier this year, the wind and the rain tearing at us as they do, and my sisters [Bertha Monterney and Ruby Pem] are older than I am, much older, their dances slowing down.[71]

The image shows Bertha Monterney as a squash plant, clinging to the earth and almost reposing into decomposition, and as the novel begins with her death, this portrayal dramatizes that loss. Meanwhile, Ruby Pem's face emerges skyward from an ear of corn, evoking a birth image, as the gasoline hose and treaty belt interlock above her head, distantly resembling a skydome. Fiction Tunny's young bean vines curl and crouch, embracing Ruby above and Bertha below, a trajectory that outlines the timeframe of her closing relationship with Bertha in the prologue and budding relationship with Ruby at the novel's end. The complicated nature of the image and of Gansworth's print narrative refuse any pat conclusions about the relative good of any one definition of tradition; Mason Rollins views his own pursuit of the tobacco trade as a worthy expression of Hodinöhsö:ni' identity and treaty rights: "The treaty rights I scored big time with in my business are the same rights Bud and his family have been using for—oh, easily the last several generations. Those same treaty rights Bert ranted on and on about all through our dance practices finally came in handy for me."[72] While the confusing mass of vines, stalk, gasoline hoses, and treaty belt in this piece might imply a choking out of the Three Sisters, the title's mention of an "embrace" and Fiction's own observations about the powerful nature of these entwinements suggest that the belts and hoses' braiding is mutually constitutive and supportive of the Three Sisters and the sustenance they communicate in Hodinöhsö:ni' visual code.

"Smoke Rings," the image on the novel's title page offers a further examination of these themes, which removes the visual presence of naturalistically-drawn humans from the unfolding drama, while continually alluding to human agency in the creation of material culture and generation of revenue.

10. Eric Gansworth, "Smoke Rings," from *Smoke Dancing*. Image © Eric Gansworth, used with permission.

In this painting, Turtle stands against a background of a repeating Canandaigua Treaty Belt with the figures flanking the longhouses immediately behind it. The Tree of Peace is formed on Turtle's back from an upright cigarette as a tree trunk and smoke rings as branches; in light of the prophecy that foretells a day when the chiefs who form the branches of the Tree of Peace will hold it up as it falls, one wonders what will be left to support it. Given Bud Tunny's own participation in business ventures solely for his and his Tuscarora family's benefit, the smoke rings comment not only upon Mason's business, but also upon Bud's toxic individualism. The hydro poles on Turtle's back signify Ezekiel Tunny's original selling-out to the power companies for the reservoir; yet, as Gansworth notes, one can see the geometrical designs of the wampum themselves repeated in the metal frame of the poles. Above the Turtle, we see the trunk of the Tree of Peace is being burned at the base, implying its impending fall, and the gasoline hoses form a genetic double helix around the cigarette, and they terminate in hoses meeting in the shape of an eagle. According to prophecy, the eagle will approach to warn the people of imminent danger, a threat to the Great Peace. While this painting possesses a lower emotive charge than "Three Sisters (I): Embrace," the signifiers within it offer a layered message to the studied reader of Iroquois images, one that offers guideposts to the narrative that follows and also suggests the potential for explosion that Fiction attributes to nitrogen through the proximity of the cigarette's fire and gasoline.

The internal images within the novel, "Rabbit Dance," "Standing Quiver Dance," and "Smoke Dance," organize the novel's unfolding plot by the nature of the individual dances. The Rabbit Dance is a couple's dance, and this section of the novel is focused on couplings and hoped-for couplings between Bud Tunny and Deanna Johns, Fiction Tunny and Big Red Harmony, and Fiction and Mason Rollins.

The "Rabbit Dance" image presents one of these near-connections through Fiction's reflection reaching to a mirror that holds a male wampum figure in the outline of an eagle, again alluding to the eagle's ability to give the warning cry before danger. Beyond the wampum belt's border, the moon emerges, connecting Fiction's reach with Sky Woman. The male wampum figure potentially stands for an assortment of men

11. Eric Gansworth, "Rabbit Dance," from *Smoke Dancing*. Image © Eric Gansworth, used with permission.

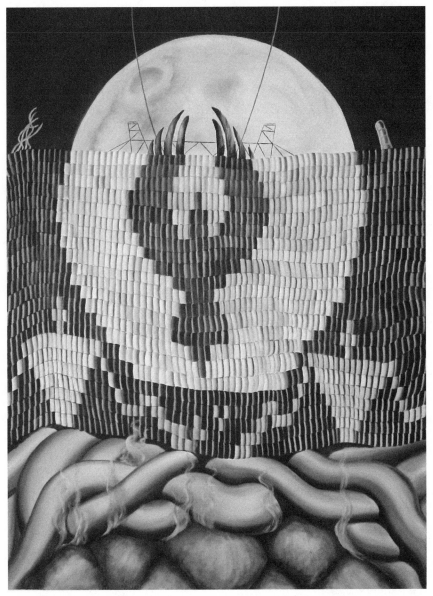

12. Eric Gansworth, "Standing Quiver Dance," from *Smoke Dancing*. Image © Eric Gansworth, used with permission.

with whom Fiction has contact (i.e., Mason, Big Red); however, the most likely candidate for her to confront in her own reflection is Bud Tunny, though this mutual recognition does not occur until the novel's end when Bud scorches his features clean in a fire. The image for "Standing Quiver Dance" carries the visual themes of the moon and wampum forward.

The Standing Quiver Dance is a dance for men leaving and returning from the hunt and for the beginning and ending of a hunter's journey. The silver chain of friendship is burnt clean at the bottom of the image, or perhaps these are entwined gasoline hoses that are about to be ignited by the smoke from burning tobacco.[73] The friendship chain in wampum seems about to break or dissolve above the silver chain, though perhaps it will simply be brightened, not destroyed. As an addition to the male friendship chain, we see a new addition to the belt, the moon with a bird, possibly a phoenix, rising from the flame, and behind the belt, we see the actual moon and the hydro lines from the reservoir at Tuscarora. In the final section of the book entitled "Smoke Dance," Gansworth takes the topic of war dances and nationalism from alphabetic print to the visual text in which we are reminded that Smoke Dance is Fiction's "specialty."[74]

Kahente Horn-Miller writes that "Where the term *wasase* ('Smoke Dance') comes from is not known, but it means renewal."[75] Thus, Fiction's role will be one of bringing new growth in the novel. The phoenix from "Standing Quiver Dance" is now revealed to be a woman, most likely Fiction, confronting the hydro lines and the loss of land they represent with the wampum belt on the left and the gas pump on the right, which asserts nationalism and sovereignty.[76] The image is at once traditionalized and innovative in interweaving seemingly disparate images and showing their interrelationship; the use of the unclothed female form highlights the great significance of women in righting historical wrongs that have occurred, while challenging Eurowestern aesthetics of the female nude.[77]

Coda: Rabbit Dance and Women's Labor at the Falls

A unique aspect of the Two Row, the Canandaigua Treaty, and the many other subsequent treaties made between them and thereafter is that they are viewed *by the Hodinöhsö:ni'* as lasting for as long as the natural world

13. Eric Gansworth, "Smoke Dance," from *Smoke Dancing*. Image © Eric Gansworth, used with permission.

continues its regular and observable processes (i.e., flowing water/grass growth moving in circles). In fact, the European and American signatories to these treaties *also agreed to these terms* with the explicit language that was a part of all such international agreements. Further, as time continued, the United States would occasionally restate its affirmation of the veracity of these original words and understandings of sovereign nation-to-nation relationships between the Hodinöhsö:ni' and the United States. For example, the right to trade on privately owned land at Niagara Falls was guaranteed by General Peter B. Porter to the Tuscaroras after a number of Tuscarora men rescued him during the War of 1812. Brian Printup and Neil Patterson Jr. write that "the Porter family gave the Tuscarora women the right to sell their beadwork in perpetuity on their land along the Niagara rapids. In 1885, the Porter land became known as Prospect Park, and Tuscaroras continue to sell beadwork to the international visitors."[78] This agreement originally affirmed Tuscarora rights to sell trade items in the boundaries of the original Niagara Reservation, which no longer exists outside of the Niagara Reservation Park, which is maintained by the city of Niagara Falls.[79] Over time, infractions were made into Hodinöhsö:ni' rights to trade in the park, a right largely exercised by Six Nations women who sold beadwork there; in fact, the Porter agreement likely served to vouchsafe an original treaty right of free trade across international boundaries, which women from Buffalo Creek Territory and surrounding communities were no longer able to exercise. In 1936, the trade was completely stopped; however, in the same year, the state moved to instituting a lottery that distributes a set number of permits to a limit of five Native American beadworkers.[80]

While the annual granting of licenses to Tuscarora women to trade their goods tax-free at Niagara Falls might appear to be an anomaly to the untrained eye, these annual licenses *and their continued issuing* represent a distinct, overt, and clear acknowledgement of original rights guaranteed Hodinöhsö:ni' peoples in numerous treaties, especially the Canandaigua and Jay Treaties. Not surprisingly, Eric Gansworth represents this tradition in his play *Rabbit Dance* (2011) via the characters of Rhoda and Flossie Door who enact treaty rights onstage, affirming Hodinöhsö:ni' epistemic traditions and sovereign rights to trade freely throughout Six Nations territories.[81] Gansworth's play, moreover, performs an economic critique that is rooted in Six Nations' sovereign status and that demands his audience members problematize the economy of treaty creation, agreement, and abrogation, a series of functions that too often result in American Indian poverty and its associated ills. By raising questions of "haves" and "have-nots," Gansworth deepens audience members' understanding of the depth of Native North American loss *and* implicates them in resolving these social inequities through the play's emplotment.

Rabbit Dance depicts the chance entwinement of four women's lives: Rhoda Door, a Tuscarora beadworker; her daughter Crystal, now deceased; Rhoda's mother Flossie, also a beadworker; and Myna, a young non-Native woman.[82] Myna's visit to Rhoda and Flossie's beadwork tables at the falls prompts a re-telling and ceremonial "fixing" of Crystal's untimely death at the hands of her abusive boyfriend, Cameron. Myna especially needs to hear this story, as she is plagued by her boyfriend Eddie's escalating control and abuse. Meanwhile, her father's obliviousness to this threat to his daughter, and Myna's mother's absence due to her early death, leave Myna with no mature (female) guidance in relationships; in fact, Rhoda and Flossie manage to intervene and potentially save Myna from continuing the destructive path her relationship with Eddie seems about to take her on.

Rabbit Dance performs an economic critique of twenty-first century Tuscarora living conditions utilizing a framework grounded in treaty rights and labor, and it extends the covenant chain to provide for the unique status of the Porter agreement, affirming the veracity and continuance of the treaties as binding agreements. Gansworth's production notes emphasize that the beadwork vendors bring tables with them everywhere; in fact, Flossie's difficulty carrying these heavy items given her disability and age is duly noted in dialogue. Moreover, "each woman, if she is sitting at the table, idly engages in creating new beadwork," illustrating the unending nature of this work.[83] Additionally, Flossie and Rhoda themselves comment repeatedly upon their labor in producing beadwork for vending, providing the distinct impression that treaty rights are serious business and that these women uphold them *in spite* of the physical toll it takes, not because the licenses provide them with a venue that is effortless to reach and from which to sell their goods. When questioned by Myna about the Germans' penchant for Tuscarora beadwork, Flossie conjectures, "Maybe they admire our survival skills." Further, Rhoda lays bare the economic struggle of those few women lucky enough to win a license as she waxes romantic about fiscal solvency: "You pray for a German day, all April and May, when times are tight, and you're down to your last hanks of beads, you make the most perfect Victorian boot pincushion you can, give it loops, satin trimming, raised roses, and fantasize about German tourists coming your way."[84] Interestingly, Rhoda's narrative substitutes the romance of a relationship for the romance of economic solvency, a rhetorical gesture that informs the plays plot; meanwhile, Flossie, who is both older and more experienced, is not seduced by either fantasy.

The raw economic realities of reservation life are highlighted by Flossie's poor health, which have resulted in her diabetes and progressive loss of vision.[85] A federal and state failure to provide Tuscarora tribal citizens with adequate healthcare in spite of their sovereign status weakens Flossie's ability to survive economically. The stereotypes of impoverished, criminal Indians have not been lost on Myna who worries that Flossie will steal her phone, though Flossie assures her that she "make[s] enough on any given day to buy three of those stupid phones."[86] Meanwhile, Rhoda and Flossie sell their work to raise money for a memorial to "women who have sold beadwork at the brink of the falls since before it was a state park" and to the memory of Crystal.[87] Rhoda is quoted in the newspaper article as saying: "We've been doing this longer than there's been a park here. When this was private land, owned by the Porter family, we got rights to continue selling beadwork to tourists forever from the Porters, for our men having protected General Peter Porter during the War of 1812. Since it got turned into a park in 1885, we've had to fight to maintain our rights, though it seems like that white family who owns the Maid of the Mist doesn't have to fight to keep their private business going in the middle of a state park."[88]

The memorial to the women beadworkers and to Crystal operates as a counterpoint to the Maid of the Mist and Crystal's boyfriend's enactment of this white myth in his murder of her.[89] Flossie worries whether the "next generation might forget. . . . If they can remember Tesla, they can remember a young Indian woman who found her own beauty despite what her boyfriend did to her, right up to the end."[90] In this way, the women's artistic generation at the falls counteracts the damage of dominant stereotypes of Indian male rage that covers over the latent and active violence of conquest perpetrated by non-Native men.

The three texts by Eric Gansworth that I have discussed all perform differing and converging economic critiques that are rooted in treaty rights, specifically the Canandaigua Treaty as well as the Jay Treaty and earlier treaties. As each text in the chain enlightens us in differing ways, so too do we reach a new understanding of the original friendships and agreements that they stand for. Gansworth's fiction, poetry, drama, and paintings engage the Canandaigua Treaty Belt and other friendship belts as part of the formulation and expression of a Hodinöhsö:ni' aesthetic; perhaps even more importantly, Gansworth ties the storying of this treaty to the material conditions his characters face in their daily struggles for "survival money" and the concomitant promises of treaty agreements.

As this essay has established, Gansworth reads the Canandaigua Treaty Belt as tying whites into the Iroquois Confederacy through the image of entwined hands that link non-Natives and Natives in the Ironormative political and economic understandings of the land. Patricia Albers has cautioned against "unwittingly reproduc[ing] frameworks that segregate Native American labor from the rest of the economy and portray it in isolating terms";[91] in fact, the goal of this essay has been to present a capacious frame for reading the Native North American economy within Indigenous epistemology. Gansworth's renditions of the Canandaigua Treaty Belt provide a map for navigating this new ecogeospatial relationship between settler and Indigene, a cartography in which a Hodinöhsö:ni' worldview is still normative. In the Iroquois economy, common boundaries and spaces are regularly invoked spatially and ceremonially: the commons, the fields, and the edge of the woods. This essay contributes to larger efforts in working-class and Indigenous knowledge production, and answers the call to account for the land in contemporary economics and to include Indigenous knowledge of that land as part of the formulation. The friendship belt and Gansworth's representations of it within literary works both account for the absence of land *and* its value in working-class studies and suggest how it might be incorporated into a critique of capitalism *and* responsible contemporary economic development in Indigenous territories.

3

Tribal Feminist Recuperation of the Mother of Nations in Shelley Niro's *Kissed by Lightning*

A Rematriating Reading of the Women's Nomination Belt

> This is . . . called the Women's Nomination Belt, and this is what was given to the clanmothers. . . . it acknowledged the role of the women in the Confederacy and the relationship to the land.
>
> —Beverley Jacobs (Mohawk Nation, Bear Clan)[1]

In roughly AD 1142 a Wendat man paddled across Lake Ontario in a white stone canoe.[2] He was conceived without his mother having intercourse with a mortal man, "a divine birth" of auspicious circumstances that was foretold by in a dream brought by a messenger from the Great Spirit to his grandmother.[3] He came across Lake Ontario bearing a message of peace, but he was born with a deformity of the mouth that prevented clear speech. In some versions, this is a cleft lip; in others, it is a "double row of teeth,"[4] which is how Dewaseráge Chief William D. Loft (Mohawk) translates the Peacemaker's name.[5] The first person he approached with the Good News of Peace and Power was a woman who lived along the warpath and who fed the warriors as they made their treks to and from battles, feeding the never-ending cycle of violence that characterized Seneca, Cayuga, Onondaga, Oneida, and Mohawk society at that time. When she decided to accept his message, she concomitantly chose to cease feeding the warriors who stopped to eat at her home beside the warpath.[6] The Peacemaker gave her the name Jigonsaseh [Jegöhsase:'] or "New Face," "for [her] countenance evinces the New Mind."[7] The Peacemaker imparted to her the new social order or way of the mind that he carried, in which people's lives would be organized around longhouses where one clanmother would predominate. The Mother of Nations agreed to all this, but was concerned that her decision alone would not be enough to withstand the tidal force of rage and grief that fed perpetual war. The Peacemaker went farther eastward, meeting Ha:yëwënta' who was himself grieving the loss of his wife and daughters. Helping Ha:yëwënta' to condole his dead through the use of wampum, the Peacemaker continued eastward until he met with the great cannibal, Tadodahoh, who refused to hear his message; so horrific was Tadodahoh that his hair was a mass of writhing snakes, signifying his disordered mind. Undaunted, the Peacemaker and Ha:yëwënta' traveled to the Mohawks, Oneidas, Cayugas, and Senecas, spreading the Good News of Peace and Power, until only Tadodahoh was left unchanged. They returned to him and eventually won him to the new way, and Ha:yëwënta' combed the snakes from Tadodahoh's hair, earning him his name that means "he who combs."[8]

Some important aspects of the Hodinöhsö:ni' ("People of the Longhouse") politico-social structure that resulted from these events include the following: clanmothers were to install and dehorn chiefs; clanmothers were to hold and keep names for chiefs and other individuals, as names belong to clans and are held in a basket by clanmothers; individual clans were organized around three to eight animals, depending on the Hodinöhsö:ni' nation; wampum and the condolence ceremony were given to Ha:yëwënta' during his grieving for his family at the falls at Onondaga Lake; and each Nation was afforded a set number of chiefs, with the Onondagas retaining the highest number and the supreme chief position of Tadodahoh. In brief, the Peacemaker bestowed an entire social order, which would comprise a book-length study unto itself and has inspired numerous studies from Morgan, Norton, Hewitt, and Fenton, to Parker, Johansen, Mann, and Rice.

Numerous renditions of this epic exist, each emphasizing different aspects of the story. Significantly, the Mother of Nations often plays a less prominent role in many versions of this history, although her decisive acts are clearly pivotal in other versions.[9] The Senecas are the ones who most remember her significant role, generally speaking, for although each nation comprising the Six Nations possesses different relationships to her, her village at Ganondagan sits squarely in Seneca Territory: her tribal identity was most likely Neutral or Tobacco (i.e., Attiwendaronk), as both groups were absorbed by the Senecas.[10] Perhaps the obvious reason for the progressive de-emphasis of the Mother of Nations' role in retellings of these events is erosion of matrilocal and matrifocal knowledges and narrative since the first Hodinöhsö:ni' contact with Europeans in the 1530s during Cartier's expedition. Barbara Alice Mann offers the following statement about the Mother of Nations' significance and remembrance:

> As his very first step towards establishing peace, the Peacemaker sought out . . . the New Face of Corn—the Lynx, who had also returned [like Sapling, whom Mann connects with the Peacemaker] in the people's time of need. An emissary, herself, originally from the Attiwendaronks (Neutral Wyandots) come to spread the message of corn, she was the leader of the Cultivators with whom the Peacemaker had to deal if he hoped to prevail. . . .
>
> Together, the Peacemaker, the [J——], and *Ayonwatha* proved invincible, persuading the warring nations, one by one, to throw down their arms. . . . In a ploy suggested by the [J——], the peace trio confronted *Adodaroh* in body with all their supporters from all the nations, silently encircling him, thus dramatically demonstrating to him the strength of the peace movement.[11]

Mann's comments are illustrative of how dramatically the centrality of the Mother of Nations may differ from varying versions of the Great Law. For instance, Tom Porter's version of the Great Law cites her as an important agent and potential obstacle; however, her activity in the dissemination of the Great Law ceases once she herself has accepted it. Further, her character in Porter's version is highly manipulative, controlling, and sexually calculating.[12] This negative characterization in Porter's version may reflect European influence in the epic's transmission, as well as support the rationale for a tribal feminist rematriation of the Mother of Nations.[13]

This essay explores a specific retelling of the Peacemaker epic that both reinstalls the Mother of Nations in her central role in this history and endeavors a tribal feminist recuperation of this narrative in which a woman is written into Tadodahoh's role. In her 2009 film, *Kissed by Lightning,*

Shelley Niro (Turtle Clan, Bay of Quinté Mohawk) casts the Mother of Nations, Ha:yëwënta', and the Peacemaker in a contemporary setting with present-day identities that maintain historical resonances of the memorialized past: the Mother of Nations' contemporary corollary is Mavis Dogblood, a solitary painter; Ha:yëwënta' is Bug King, Mavis's friend and now lover; and the Peacemaker is Jesse Lightning, her now-deceased husband. In this essay, I argue that *Kissed by Lightning* figuratively reads the Women's Nomination Belt by recounting the Mother of Nations' critical acts in accepting and propagating the Great Law of Peace creatively and contemporarily. Further, I situate this reading around several key moments in the film that speak to the larger body of Niro's work, thereby suggesting that her portrait of the Mother of Nations and this foundational Hodinöhsö:ni' narrative emanates from a tribal feminist (i.e., Hodinöhsö:ni'-specific) theoretical praxis and aesthetic. Finally, by considering the significance of the women's nomination belt and its application to treaty protocol, I read the Phelps and Gorham Purchase at Buffalo Creek (1788) and the Buffalo Creek Treaties (1838, 1842) as comparative examples of the progressive retreat of women's roles in Seneca (and Six Nations) public political processes, which now are becoming more highly visible again through actions taken at Caledonia, Ontario, and Six Nations' participation in Idle No More. I construct this reading as an extension of Deborah Doxtator's conceptual work on Godi'Nigoha', the Women's Mind, an Iroquois intellectual tradition that has been obscured by heteropatriarchy. Doxtator observes that "our Iroquois minds have disappeared along with the cornfields, or at the very least been wiped clean."[14] As the bringer of the corn culture (and the Great Law of Peace), the Mother of Nations' erasure is dramatically illustrated in the uncultivated cornfields, much as Godi'Nigoha' has been obscured through forced acculturation in residential and boarding schools. This essay is an intervention in that process and a reclamation of Godi'Nigoha' and the Mother of Nations through a reading of the Women's Nomination Belt in Shelley Niro's *Kissed by Lightning*.

Shelley Niro is a Bay of Quinté Mohawk, Turtle Clan, who was born in Niagara Falls in 1954 and raised between that city and Ohswéken, Six Nations. Niro earned her BFA in painting and sculpture from the Ontario College of Art in 1990 and her MFA from the University of Western

Ontario in 1997, and she lives in Brantford near Six Nations. In addition to *Kissed by Lightning* (2009), her first feature-length film, which is the focus of this essay, Niro's filmography includes a wealth of short experimental films: *It Starts with a Whisper* (1992), co-directed with Anna Gronau; *Overweight with Crooked Teeth* (1997); *Honey Moccasin* (1998); *Pensarosa* (2001); *Midwinter Dreams* (2002); *The Shirt* (2003); *Suite: Indian* (2005); *Tree* (2007); *Rechargin'* (2007); *The Flying Head* (2008); and *Hunger* (2008). Additionally, Niro recently directed a documentary on Salteaux painter and scholar Robert Houle, entitled *Robert's Paintings* (2011). Her films have been honored with awards from the Red Earth Festival, Dreamspeakers Festival, Two Rivers Festival, Wind and Glacier Festival, and Santa Fe Film Festival, and she has held an Eiteljorg Fellowship, in addition to winning grants from Women in Film and Sparkplug programs. Niro's painting, photography, sculpture, and beadwork have been exhibited widely both domestically and internationally; her works have been collected in museums throughout Canada, the United States, and Germany. As Lee-Ann Martin notes, Niro "moves easily among multiple media—photography, poetry, film, beadwork, painting, sculpture, and storytelling"—though she is best known for her photography (i.e., *Mohawks in Beehives* (1991) and *This Land Is Mime Land* (1992)) and her films.[15] Martin further elaborates, "Her art emerges in the tension between honoring ancestral traditions and acknowledging the right to find daring and innovative ways to proceed into the future. Niro acknowledges the need to incorporate traditional elements into her art while continually challenging herself to be inventive."[16] In *Kissed by Lightning* and other works, Niro incorporates wampum belts and their attendant knowledges (or newly encoded knowledges in new belts) into the visual code of her filmic and photo aesthetic.

Similarly, in a very specific way, Niro recuperates the Mother of Nations' cultural contributions and the Women's Nomination Belt that testifies to her achievements into the multiple layers of images (film, painting, beadwork) of *Kissed by Lightning*.

There is little one could say to overestimate the importance of clan-mothers in Hodinöhsö:ni' society. Foundational to Iroquois identity is the transmission of nation and clan from one's mother; without a Hodinöhsö:ni'

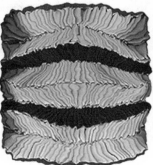

14. In "Parallel Worlds of Women," Shelley Niro uses the dual vision of the photographic stereograph as a way of exploring the roles played by a little-known French World War I heroine, Mlle. Marcelle Semmer, and a doubly obscured (by race *and* gender) Mother of Nations (the Lynx). Reprinted with permission of the artist.

mother, one is not fully Hodinöhsö:ni' nor does one inherit a clan. Adoption (or, in Iroquois, "hanging a name around one's neck") is the only route to gaining full citizenship in these cases. Fathers play a tertiary role in a child's upbringing, traditionally, while maternal uncles are much more prominent and enact what would be understood as a more fatherly role in a Eurowestern sense, in terms of teaching appropriate boundaries for proper behavior. Traditional Hodinöhsö:ni' society was matrifocal and matrilocal with each longhouse being run by one head matron and her sisters and daughters assisting. Married couples lived at the wife's mother's longhouse, and men were cyclically and consistently away for hunting and fishing, only living in the longhouse during occasional respites from this movement tied to the ceremonial year and to working with women in the fields. In a Eurowestern sense, then, women owned the home, the fields, and the food; even the game that men hunted was surrendered to their wives and clanmothers for their judicial distribution. In an economy centered on women's ownership and distribution of food, women decided when and how men would go to war. Women, in fact, performed nearly all major decisions pertinent to daily life, and the longhouse economy depended upon their good judgment regarding proper courses of action.[17]

The Mother of Nations is understood as the first clanmother in a new Hodinöhsö:ni' Confederacy wrought by the Peacemaker, transmitted by

Ha:yëwënta', and accepted by the Mother of Nations, first and foremost. It should be understood that clanmothers existed prior to the Peacemaker; however, he endowed them with specific functions in the new sociopolitical order, much as he did chiefs. The Mother of Nations' home village was Ganondagan, which also was the national granary for the Senecas.[18] In terms of bare economics, if women held power based on or residing in their control of food, then the Mother of Nations was of the utmost importance, as her food storage was the largest in the Seneca Nation at the time. Oral traditions carried by Peter Jemison and other Senecas affirm Ganondagan's critical importance to survival and the Mother of Nations' concomitant centrality as the head matron of that village; in fact, the importance of Senecas to the Confederacy is likely predicated upon the Mother of Nations' identity as Seneca. Written records from the Denonville (1687) and Sullivan-Clinton (1779) campaigns affirm the size and scope of the corn and vegetable stores at Ganondagan; thus, the role of historic Mother of Nations spanned her lifetime (circa AD 1142) and multiple centuries after her passing from the physical plane.

There are several Hodinöhsö:ni' wampum belts that record agreements internal to the Six Nations. The Ha:yëwënta' Belt records the agreement of the Five Nations to enter into a confederacy depicted as a longhouse with the Senecas as the Keepers of the Western Door, the Onondagas as Keepers of the Central Fire, and the Mohawks as Keepers of the Eastern Door. The Three Sisters Belt records the important relationship of these Life Sustainers in the Hodinöhsö:ni' agricultural economy, and it depicts the corn, beans, and squash abstractly as three groupings or corn hills formed of three white diamonds on a background of purple. Thus, the belt records the balance created in the nitrogen count of the soil by planting these three companion plants together. The Women's Nomination Belt, which is the subject of this essay, records the clanmothers' authority to select, install, and dehorn chiefs. The belt depicts six individuals linking hands over four small squares in the middle; thus, three figures in purple wampum flank the fire on either side on a background of white wampum.

The human figures are the clanmothers (Iotiianehshon), and the lines connecting them denote their responsibility to regulate names and other

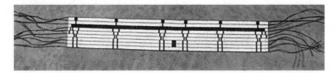

15. The Women's Nomination Belt: reproduction design by
Ken Maracle. Photograph by Raymond Skye. Courtesy of
Ken Maracle, www.wampumshop.com.

functions. That the lines and figures are placed on a white background illustrates that the clanmothers are "the holders of the Kariwiio (Good Message), Kashastensera (Power) and Skennen (Peace)." The squares in the middle represent the two sides of Younger and Elder Brother, before which any candidates selected by a clanmother to be chief must stand for examination or scrutiny.[19]

Mavis Dogblood, the central character in Shelley Niro's Kissed by Lightning, allegorizes the originary figure of the Mother of Nations; more importantly, her personal struggles dramatize walking the path to acceptance of the Peacemaker's message for any individual in a contemporary setting. Hence, her personal transformation models how a given individual might translate "traditional" tribal knowledges into the present context. Because she finally refuses bitterness and the desire for revenge in favor of forgiveness and inner peace, Mavis/Mother of Nations makes possible the recovery from war and violence of the Hodinöhsö:ni' as a whole; because Mavis has a present-day identity, her ceremonial enactment of accepting the Great Law has the potential to initiate cultural rebirth on a wide-scale.

Mavis's struggles in Kissed by Lightning largely stem from her ensuing grief after the loss of her husband, Jesse Lightning, through a freak accident in which he is struck by lightning while playing his viola along the river.[20] Niro's directorial decision to place Mavis (Mother of Nations) and Jesse (Peacemaker) in a romantic relationship is not without precedent: Barbara Mann notes, "Some of the Senecas and Wyandots say that the Peacemaker and the [Mother of Nations] wed."[21] Jesse's viola playing suggests that part of the Peacemaker's message surpasses the ability of language to provide peace: in fact, Jesse comments upon how he always hears music and is overwhelmed by the rapture it produces. Wampum itself, likewise, both

16. Mavis Dogblood, played by Kateri Walker, painting her "Peacemaker" series in *Kissed by Lightning*. Courtesy of Shelley Niro.

functions "as words," as Wallace states, and surpasses language's finite nature in its ability to transmit messages, especially that of the Great Law of Peace. Mavis is surrounded by wampum: she wears it; she portrays it in paintings; she adorns her artist's studio with it.[22]

Although she carries the stories told her by Jesse, and although she has the tools to transform (i.e., wampum), she is held back by her deep grief over the loss of Jesse. Rather than facing her own grief, rage, and desperation, Mavis wallows in depression, and fails to stand up for herself or others when preyed upon. For instance, Jesse's first wife, Kateri (also Tadodahoh) asks to move into Mavis's home, and Mavis obliges, but moves next door into her artist's studio. Mavis views her responsibility for caring for Jesse's surviving family members, Kateri, and her son Zeus, whose father was Jesse, as mere "obligations." In essence, Mavis performs her service to Jesse after his death as a matter of form, not as a matter of empathy. She fulfills her duty, in a Hodinöhsö:ni' sense, by taking care of relations in the tribal web of community; however, she does not do so in the right spirit and continues to hold Kateri, Zeus, and her friend Bug/ Ha:yëwënta' at a distance. Highlighting the complexity of how the path to Peace unfolds, Mavis fulfills her "Lightning obligation" on the drive to

New York by stopping to see Josephine Lightning, Jesse's mother, in order to drop off photos for Kateri. Ultimately, Josephine provides the transformative context for Mavis to finally accept Peace into her heart and to abandon her grief, as the conception scene with Bug in the bedroom suggests.

One of the unique elements in Niro's tribal feminist narrative is the gender transposition of Tadodahoh from a male Onondaga chief to a Mohawk woman (Kateri) who is the first wife of the now-dead Jesse Lightning. Kateri's character is marked by a series of pronounced flaws: her greed, which leads her to usurp nearly everything that Mavis owns (i.e., house, car, clothes); her blindness, which is exemplified by her dismissal of Jesse's and her son Zeus's musical talents (i.e., "All he [Jesse] cared about was playing that stupid violin"); her internal colonization, which is communicated through her devotion to Kateri Tekakwitha and the Catholic church. Niro goes so far as to dress Kateri in enormous hair rollers that visually mimic the snakes in Tadodahoh's hair.

The casting of the Mother of Nations and Tadodahoh as widows of the same husband highlights the deeply personal nature of the message of Peace and Power; moreover, reframing the story in a woman's context outside of the chiefs' roles, which are predicated originally upon the clanmothers' installment, draws light to often-overlooked women's political traditions beyond selection and installment of chiefs, such as women's councils, which were (and are) solely the province of Hodinöhsö:ni' women.[23] The pivotal role of Tadodahoh is rooted in women's power, and Niro's casting of Tadodahoh as a woman emphasizes the source of this power. Further, making the Mother of Nations/Mavis and Tadodahoh/Kateri primary to the narrative emphasizes the importance of women in the acceptance, dissemination, and implementation of the Great Law of Peace, a practice that is maintained today in the duties officiated by clanmothers.[24]

Niro emphasizes the cooperative relationship between the Peacemaker and Ha:yёwёnta' in the propagation of the Great Law of Peace in Mavis's relationships to firstly, Jesse, and secondly, Bug. Jesse tells Mavis the story of the Peacemaker and Ha:yёwёnta' repeatedly during his lifetime, and his final composition is the Hiawatha Sonata, anticipating the role that Bug/Ha:yёwёnta' will play in ongoing efforts to communicate the need for Peace. First, Jesse, and later, Bug, try to emphasize the relevance

17. Kateri, played by Rachelle White Wind Arbez, knocks on Mavis's trailer door in *Kissed by Lightning*. Courtesy of Shelley Niro.

and pertinence of the Peacemaker's message to Mavis: Mavis remembers Jesse saying, "this story took place *here*" as she and Bug drive through Mohawk Territory to the Kateri Tekakwitha Shrine, and after their stop, Bug points to the landscape, stating, "Ha:yëwënta', Peacemaker, Tadodahoh, the waterfalls, everything is right *here*." Art historian Neal Keating observes that in Niro's work, "memory resides in the land, especially in the woods and along the rivers."[25]

Jesse's stories inform Mavis's painting, her waking life, and her dreams; however, Bug is the necessary messenger who helps Mavis to fully accept this message into her life in the wake of her grieving for Jesse. Josephine Lightning plays a pivotal role in helping Mavis condole Jesse and accept her life (and Peace) thereafter; she teases Mavis: "do you think it was *an accident* that you got lost?"

In a parallel example of necessary messaging, Shanna Sabbath must be visited by her grandfather, Elijah Harper, in Niro's *It Starts with a Whisper* (1993); Elijah warns Shanna against "too much thinking" (Euro-Canadian thought) and invites her "to live your own life" and not wallow in grief for those individuals who have passed, such as the Tuteloes. Shanna's own aunts have tried to impart this wisdom of not obsessing about

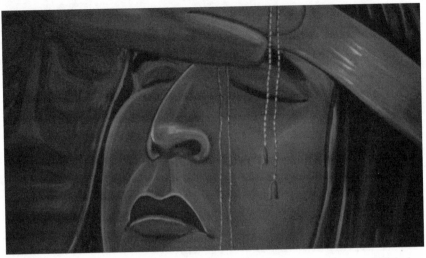

18. "The Healing of Touch," an original painting by Shelley Niro featured in her film *Kissed by Lightning*, depicts Ha:yëwënta' in mourning. Courtesy of Shelley Niro.

the mainstream media's misrepresentations of First Nations people; however, Shanna personally needs to receive this message from her grandfather, an acceptance that is marked by spiritual dimensions visually, as is the conception scene in *Kissed by Lightning*.

The river, another culturally charged trope, also recurs in *Kissed by Lightning* and other work by Niro. In *Kissed by Lightning*, the river is the location where Jesse is struck by lightning as he plays his viola, taking him away, at least physically, from Mavis. In the dream-memory sequences during which Mavis grieves for Jesse, they are separated by a frozen river, which she reaches over and calls for him. When she is finally able to release him during her visit with Josephine Lightning, she dreams of waving goodbye to Jesse over the river, and awakens to fully embracing Bug, who no longer needs to wipe away her tears; in fact, the visual motif of chiefs' horns in the beadwork hanging in the scene suggest the spiritual work of wampum in condolence as well as the baby they will conceive and who represents the coming generation of Hodinöhsö:ni' leaders.[26]

Rivers figure prominently throughout Niro's other work, and the river in *The Shirt* (2001) refers to consistently violated treaties ("as long as the rivers flow"), hydroelectric projects, and Niro's own nostalgia for the Niagara River growing up in Niagara Falls. In *It Starts with a Whisper* and in her photography, Niro portrays Tutela Heights at Grand River where the surviving Tuteloes, who emigrated from Virginia northward and found "blanket protection" with the Six Nations, lived. This space along the Grand River becomes a repository of memory where Shanna (and Niro) returns to connect with ancestral loss and rebirth; Shanna's return to the Niagara River on New Year's Eve, 1992, allows her to condole the Tuteloes and other decimated tribal nations and move forward freed from her own survivor guilt.[27] The move from the Grand River to the Niagara River brings Shanna back to the heart of Six Nations Territory and figuratively undoes the Hodinöhsö:ni' retreat into Canada after the Revolutionary War. Further, Niagara Falls is very near Buffalo Creek, a Six Nations reservation that was illegally acquired through the corrupt treaty of 1838; Shanna's position overlooking the falls signifies her position at the brink of the greatest possible land theft and the greatest possible exercise of sovereignty through Confederacy council in treaties. As Michelle Raheja argues in *Reservation Reelism*, "Niagara Falls itself constitutes a virtual reservation, as it is both sacred territory to Native Americans and a dominant culture constructed tourist space, both a location of transformation and the shedding of old selves."[28]

While Mavis suffers at great expense personally and takes considerable time to receive and accept the Great Law of Peace, she herself is the vehicle for communicating the Gayaneshä'go:wa:h to her home community and to the outside world via her paintings. Mavis's exhibit in New York City is composed exclusively of images that portray the Peacemaker's journey and individuals whose lives are/were touched by his message.[29] In fact, her painting of Jesse's grandmother Josephine is completed before Mavis meets her in the temporal unfolding of the film. The striking similarity between the old woman in Mavis's painting and Josephine Lightning imply the timelessness of these central Hodinöhsö:ni' narratives, and the potential for prophecy, as examined by Danika Medak-Saltzman.[30]

To return to a pivotal point in *Kissed by Lightning*, the morning scene at Josephine Lightning's house shows Mavis clutching Jesse's baby photo album as she sleeps, only to dream of bidding her final farewell to him over the river. Her awakening to Bug, who is concerned for her tears, quickly turns into Mavis refusing his attempts to calm her. She instead chooses to embrace him fully and to trace the outlines of his face, suggesting her reciprocal care for him. As light emanates between them in the room, the camera pans to a black velvet beadwork hanging on the wall that includes chiefs' horns and the skydome. As in *It Starts with a Whisper*, Niro here uses the chiefs' horns to communicate the fulfillment of condolence in this scene: Mavis is finally able to let go of her memories of Jesse and assist in raising up the new generation of chiefs.[31]

Mavis no longer clings to her own grief and stops refusing to assist others around her, including Kateri and her son Zeus. As part of portraying this spiritual closure and regeneration, the film closes with a pregnant Mavis bearing the new generation of leadership who will support and protect the Great Peace. Mavis, whose surname is Dogblood, has moved from the need for blood revenge, however metaphorically, to the ability to transform her wounds into new life; Bug, in turn, has been successful in helping Mavis to accept the Great Law and will now presumably turn to aiding Kateri/Tadodahoh in her transformation.

In *Writing from a Red Zone*, Patricia Hilden considers the demands of centering American Indian narratives in Indigenous frameworks; furthermore, she outlines the need for Indigenous feminist interventions in current scholarship:

> I see the Red Zone as a shifting field, as, in Robin D. G. Kelley's words, a "zone of engagement; not the product of bloodlines or some essence all Indians possess". . . .
>
> The second, though no less vital, zone is that of feminism. . . . This second zone, then, is a zone-within-a-zone, informed by continuing, and often radically different, oppressions suffered by women both within and without the indigenous world.[32]

In *Kissed by Lightning*, Shelley Niro performs a tribal feminist intervention in Peacemaker/Ha:yëwënta'/Mother of Nations narratives by both reintroducing the Mother of Nations as central to this foundational story *and* reconfiguring the narrative by recasting Tadodahoh as a woman.

In fact, the leap to consider Tadodahoh in a woman's role is small, and the rationale for doing so is quite clear, given the mother-right basis of Hodinöhsö:ni' cultural and political structure. Rather than introducing extrinsic elements into the Mother of Nations/Peacemaker story, Niro instead raises the stakes for considering the implications of this foundational narrative by performing an act of recovery that draws further attention to itself by self-consciously feminizing the entire structure.

Niro's complex and sophisticated re-introduction of familiar elements in the Great Law of Peace works to recuperate Hodinöhsö:ni' women's roles and the value placed upon them. Her work has implications for pragmatic considerations, such as treaty rights, and the involvement and entwinement of wampum through *Kissed by Lightning* alludes to this intersection. Women's involvement in political processes is codified in the Great Law and the foundational role played by the Mother of Nations, and we can see this prominent role still at work publicly in the 1788 Phelps and Gorham Purchase at Buffalo Creek. Though all land sales at this date were supposed to be made through the federal government, Oliver Phelps and Nathaniel Gorham had secured the right of pre-emption from the State of Massachusetts and attempted to directly negotiate with the Six Nations at Buffalo Creek. While the Hodinöhsö:ni' at Buffalo Creek were confounded by the use of these intermediaries in lieu of federal representatives, they were persuaded to negotiate with the two men for lands east of the Genesee River. Of tantamount importance are the signatures of seven clanmothers on the purchase papers, which testify to the prominent role played by women's council and clanmothers in this land sale.

Contrastively, these signatures and those of all chiefs duly appointed by clanmothers would be missing from the Buffalo Creek Treaties of 1838 and 1842, both notoriously corrupt and secured through bribes, alcohol, and illness. Of the Buffalo Creek Treaty of 1838, William Fenton writes:

> The disastrous consequences of setting aside the unanimity principle of the confederacy were sadly developed in this treaty. [Note: The federal agents forced this violation of procedure; in fact, the unanimity principle would have guaranteed that no treaty would have been ratified without consensus.] Fifteen sixteenths of the people were opposed to

it, irreconcilably, throughout the eight years' struggle by which it was effected; and only forty-one of the eighty-one whom the Company would admit to be chiefs, by all their arts and appliances, [could] be induced to sign it. Besides, the Indians justly contended that ten or more others had an unquestionable right, by the customs of the Iroquois, to be regarded as chiefs and *that the voice of the warriors and the women could, on no account, be disregarded* [emphasis mine]. Strong protests against the treaty were therefore forwarded to the government, before its ratification . . . , [yet] the treaty was ratified.[33]

Despite the outspoken protests of Hodinöhsö:ni' clanmothers and chiefs, the Buffalo Creek Treaty (1838) and Compromise (1842) were ratified by the US Congress, and these lands were, in effect, stolen from the Six Nations. Nonetheless, women's prominence and singular importance in land transactions are evident throughout the historic record, and they affirm the responsibility recorded in the Women's Nomination Belt. The Buffalo Creek Treaty and the silencing of the women's voices in the 1830s and 1840s have not passed unnoticed; the Seneca Nation of Indians has worked to gain recognition of this travesty through establishing the Buffalo Creek Casino in 2013. The symbolic reclamation of this territory affirms the people's memory of these events and will begin the process of restitution for these nineteenth-century acts, eventually assuring the continuance of women's roles in selecting and installing chiefs and in holding councils.

In this sense, Niro's recuperation of the role of the Mother of Nations in *Kissed by Lightning* reaffirms the importance of the women's council and the powers of the clanmothers, as codified in the Women's Nomination Belt. Furthermore, taking the film's portrayal of those responsibilities allows us to derive a tribal feminist standard for evaluating treaty protocol and for reinstituting the traditional political roles of Hodinöhsö:ni' women. Looking to more recent examples of clanmothers' public prominence in events at Oka and Caledonia, we can see the unique position women are in to assert treaty rights and their roles in negotiating and evaluating any restitution and further international agreements.

4

Kahnawake's Reclamation of Adoption Practices in Tracey Deer's Documentary and Fiction Films

Reading the Adoption Belt in a Post-Indian Act Era

It was the duty of the Cayuga Nation to formally adopt other nations when they come here following the Four Roots of Peace, so the Tuscaroras were adopted as a nation, so that made us six nations, but other nations came not as a whole nation like Delaware and Tutelos [who] were all adopted here.

—Hubert Skye (Faithkeeper, Cayuga Nation, Snipe Clan)[1]

This essay considers the relationship between the Adoption Belt, the process of adoption, and the portrayal of identity formation in the Mohawk community of Kahnawake in the films of Tracey Deer, and I argue that Mohawk director Deer's documentary and fictional films and her community activism, via a Kahnawake women's group and her publication of *The Eastern Door*, figuratively read the Adoption Belt through their insistence upon relying on parameters of identity emanating from Mohawk traditional knowledge, not colonial philosophies of separation and exclusion. Deer's films narrate the Adoption Belt as a record of sovereign knowledge and a process by which Hodinöhsö:ni' people determine what constitutes an individual community member and thereby, en masse, a Hodinöhsö:ni' nation. Rather than introducing visual reproductions of wampum belts that invite us as consumers of her films to "read the wampum," Deer's work acknowledges the traditional knowledges encoded in the Adoption Belt and systematically shows their application (or lack thereof) in the present day context of Kahnawake where an intervention is required, in Deer's formulation, in order to avoid re-instituting

81

the philosophy of separation introduced by the Indian Act. Passed into law under the administration of Duncan Campbell Scott in 1876, the Indian Act limited legal status as Indians to those individuals bearing patrilineal Indigenous descent. Even more disturbingly, the Indian Act revoked legal status from Indian women who married non-Native men: their names were removed from their Nation's band rolls; their children were legally deemed non-Native; and the women themselves were barred from living on the reserve, even in cases of divorce when women would attempt to return.[2] Further, the non-Native wives of Native men were granted status, and the children of Native men were ensured status as well.[3] The Indian Act's professed goal was the enfranchisement and civilization of First Nations citizens, and its doctrine and implementation clearly inscribe heteropatriarchy into the legal discourse of Indigenous communities where this societal structure was not the prevailing regime. The long-term impact of this act of legislation is immeasurable in its violence and intergenerational trauma, and First Nations communities still seek healing from its aftermath today.[4]

As it relates to the legacy of the Indian Act and its impact upon the Kahnawake Membership Law, Deer's work raises poignant questions about the current process by which community membership is conferred and revoked, delineating the uniquely gendered effects of this inheritance. Kahnawake community members articulate the manifold ways in which membership has been fraught with colonial anxiety and dread emanating from the Indian Act in their interviews in the Speaker's Corner segments of *Club Native*. Through the collective statements of interviewees, actors, and journalists, the Kahnawake interviewees affirm the process of adoption as a normative concept for contemporary Hodinöhsö:ni' identity formation (i.e., the acquisition of status by individuals who meet community standards for identity instead of blood quantum).

Tracey Penelope Tekahentahkhwa Deer was born in 1978 on the Kahnawake Reserve to Angela and Chester Deer, both status Kahnawake Mohawks. Deer attended the Kahnawake Survival School for her primary education and Queen of Angels Academy in Montreal for her secondary education. She earned a BA in Film Studies from Dartmouth, and soon thereafter, she began working full-time in film production. Her first film,

One More River: The Deal that Split the Cree (2005), was co-directed with Neil Diamond (Cree) and won Best Documentary at the Rendez-vous du cinema québécois. Deer has subsequently written and directed several award-winning films for Rezolution Pictures, a subsidiary of the National Film Board of Canada: *Mohawk Girls* (2005), *Club Native* (2008), and *Kanien'kehá:ka/Living the Language* (2008). All of her films have generated significant popular and critical acclaim: *Mohawk Girls* won the Alanis Obomsawin Best Documentary Award at the 2005 imagineNATIVE Film & Media Arts Festival; Deer received a Gemini Award for *Club Native* and a Gemini for Best Writing in *Club Native*, in addition to the Academy of Canadian Cinema and Television's Canada Award for best multi-cultural program, Best Documentary at the Dreamspeakers Festival, Best Canadian Film at First Peoples' Festival, and the Colin Low Award for Best Canadian Documentary at the DOXA Documentary Film Festival. She has also departed into experimental film in the short *Escape Hatch* (2007), and in 2009 she completed a pilot entitled *Mohawk Girls*, which is heavily based on *Escape Hatch*, with writer Cynthia Knight. ATPN and OMNI began televising *Mohawk Girls* as a half-hour dramatic comedy in 2013. Deer also collaborated with Knight on *Crossing the Line* (2009), a 3D short for Digital Nations, which screened at the 2010 Vancouver Olympics. Additionally, Deer has created a production company, Mohawk Princess Productions, which she uses as a platform for producing her own short fiction films. She is currently at work on two documentary film series, *Working It out Together* and *Dream Big*. In addition to her work in film, from 2008 to 2012 Deer co-owned and published *The Eastern Door*, a Kahnawake community newspaper, with her former husband, Steve Bonspiel, a Kanehsatake Mohawk.[5]

In Tracey Deer's award-winning *Club Native*, members of the Kahnawake Mohawk community collectively narrate the Adoption Belt as a record of the process by which Hodinöhsö:ni' people determine what constitutes individual community membership and national identity, while dramatizing their own extrication from Euro-Canadian principles of separation and exclusion as embodied in the Indian Act, which first worked to detribalize First Nations women on patriarchal grounds, and the Kahnawake Membership Law, which has rearticulated some of those same philosophies. This essay speaks to concerns raised by Shari Huhndorf regarding nationalist discourses and patriarchy in *Mapping the Americas*:

> [I]ndigenous nationalism . . . remains an inherently limited, contradictory mode of anticolonial resistance. . . . Nationalist criticism . . . disregards global social dynamics and colonial critique, often opposing struggles for sovereignty to the interrogation of European ideologies and practices (even though these projects . . . are inseparable in Native culture). . . . Additionally, nationalism ironically imports problematic political structures and ideologies derived from Europe. These include patriarchy as well as the relatively recent acceptance by some tribes of blood quantum and a static notion of culture as criteria for Native identity. Initially imposed by federal Indian policies, these criteria fracture indigenous communities even as they enable them to guard their boundaries.[6]

This essay analyzes the decolonizing paradigms for Kahnawake Mohawk identity and membership as put forth in Deer's *Club Native* and contends that the critique advanced by Deer's subjects delineates a mode of articulating identity that comprehensively addresses Huhndorf's critique of nationalist discourse and offers an alternative—both traditional and innovative—method for conceiving identity via Adoption Belt teachings. Further, Deer's film enacts a strategy for determining identity (via the Adoption Belt) based in Peace, Power, and Righteousness, the teachings of the Great Law of Peace, which Lina Sunseri has argued are necessary for decolonizing Hodinöhsö:ni' nationalism.[7]

Long before contact with Europeans, Hodinöhsö:ni' peoples would welcome newcomers from other tribes into the Confederacy via adoption. Historian Lori Askeland writes that

> adoption was used . . . to legitimize as full tribal members persons whose fathers (rather than their mothers) were members of the matrilinear nations of the League; to keep alive or replace deceased persons or even entire clans that had depopulated or become rapidly extinct; to provide a home for a member of a clan who was unwanted by his or her home clan; and/or to keep special knowledge alive in a clan by

cross-adopting a specialist or shaman into another clan for purposes of training other members.[8]

When a newcomer arrived as a war hostage or a visitor by her own volition, there was a waiting period during which her character would be evaluated.[9] After the observation period, if the clanmothers agreed that the candidate had reasonably acclimated to the Hodinöhsö:ni' lifeway, the individual was adopted by a family and given a nation and clan.[10] Thereafter that individual was considered Hodinöhsö:ni' and her previous identity was dead.

The Adoption (or Ransom) Belt itself is comprised of three purple diagonal lines of wampum on a background of white wampum. The diagonal lines signify "an unobstructed path, or a peaceful road of communication between . . . groups," as described by Kathryn Muller.[11] Thus, the visual code of the Adoption Belt portrays connection and peace between the adoptee and her adopted nation and clan.

Regarding the adoption ceremony, Arthur C. Parker writes in *The Life of General Ely S. Parker*:

> There are many references in 17th and 18th Century records to the adoption of captives; but this was a genuine adoption, and signified permanent inclusion in the tribes and family. But even in remote days the complimentary adoption was practiced. Notable instances of this, in Western New York history, are the cases of the sons of Louis Thomas de Joncaire, . . . his sons . . . Chauvignerie, Longueuil, and others.
>
> In the early days of Buffalo, more than one of her citizens received this complimentary expression of confidence and esteem. Among the Senecas, it has ever been a proof of friendship and trust extended only to those whites whose good-will and help they felt could be counted on.

Parker provides an extensive list of individuals adopted by the Senecas: William Clement Bryant, Rev. William D. Buck, Emma A. Buck, Charles W. Dobbins, Ada Davenport Kendall, Charles D. Marshall, Gen. Peter Buel Porter, Gen. Adrian R. Root, Frank H. Severance, George K. Staples, George L. Tucker, Charles R. Wilson, Robert P. Wilson, Rt. Rev. William D. Walker, and Mrs. William D. Walker.[12] Additionally, history provides

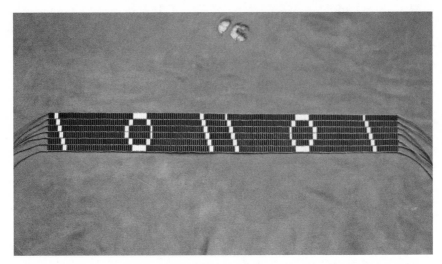

19. The Adoption (or Ransom) Belt: reproduction design by Ken Maracle. Photograph by Raymond Skye. Courtesy of Ken Maracle, www.wampumshop.com.

numerous other examples: Sir William Johnson (adopted Mohawk), Mary Jemison (adopted Seneca), John Norton (adopted Mohawk), Francesco Giuseppe Bressani (adopted Mohawk), Pierre Radisson (adopted Mohawk), and Isaac Jogues (adopted Mohawk).[13] Regarding the prevalence of adoption, Parker is careful to note that other adoptees "are not numerous, for the Senecas have never cheapened the honor by bestowing it indiscriminately, and many years sometimes elapse without the performance of the adoption rites."[14] Thus, the process of adoption is practiced with selectivity and deliberation; the decision to bring an individual into a given Hodinöhsö:ni' nation arises out of extended consideration of the best interests of the community and a given individual's ability to fit into and benefit the community's interests.

In Deer's portrayal, intervention in the status quo for membership in the Mohawk Nation at Kahnawake is needed; in *Club Native*, a community of Kahnawake interviewees perform a reading of the Adoption Belt, which offers a traditional method for incorporation of those who are not Mohawk by matrilineal descent (as understood in the Great Law) or blood quantum (as stated in the Indian Act and reified in the Kahnawake Membership Law), in a communal act of recognition of the failure of

emulating non-Indian standards for identity and community membership. Deer's film does not present the viewer with the purple and white
visual code of the Adoption Belt; however, the conversations that occur in
Club Native consistently read, articulate, and re-apply adoption protocols
as suitable solutions to the current crisis in determining membership in
the Kahnawake Band of Mohawks: Deer provides a visual narrative of
children coloring a longhouse village that reads the Adoption Belt by
bringing the viewer into a Hodinöhsö:ni' spatial imaginary. Because this
reading of the wampum belt is communal and collaborative, my methodology mirrors the collective reading of the Adoption Belt by focusing
upon the interviewees' narratives; following the exposition of the reading of the Adoption Belt, I will consider the academic discourse on this
same subject.

Club Native portrays the experiences of four Mohawk women who
must confront the grim realities of the Kahnawake Membership Law:
Sandra Sherman, daughter of a status Mohawk woman and a non-Native
man, who is originally disenfranchised under the Indian Act and continues to be denied status owing to blood quantum standards; Lauren Giles,
daughter of a status Mohawk woman and an African American man, who
is granted status by the Council of Elders during the shooting of the film;
Waneek Horn-Miller, Olympic athlete, daughter of activist Kahn-Tineta
Horn, and community role model, who chooses to partner a non-Native
Olympic swimmer, Keith; and Wahsontiiostha Tiffany Deer, Tracey Deer's
sister who chooses a non-Native partner, Andrew, and stands to lose her
status if she chooses to marry him.

Deer's documentary illustrates pragmatically how the Kahnawake
Membership Law's philosophical debt to settler definitions of Indianness
and nation are debilitating her home community. This examination of the
communal reading of the Adoption Belt in Deer's *Club Native* first considers how the centrifuge of membership functions to separate tribal people
in the cases of Sandra and Lauren, and secondly analyzes further effects
of both separation and unity that lie latent in applications of membership
enforcement to those women who partner non-Natives.

Deer begins the film with Speaker's Corner interviews of numerous
status Kahnawake Mohawks, one of whom poses the question, "What

20. *How Thick Is Your Blood?* promotional still. From left to right, Sandra Sherman, Wahsontiiostha Tiffany Deer, Lauren Giles, and Waneek Horn-Miller. Courtesy of Rezolution Productions.

exactly does it mean to be a Mohawk?" The interviewees' responses range from "I really had to think about it" to "I can't grasp . . . anything that makes me say that I'm Native, I'm a Mohawk" to "I have no idea what it means to be Mohawk."[15] Set up to critique the manner in which some band members (i.e., those with a non-Mohawk parent) must now apply for status at age 18, Deer's film seems to suggest that the correspondence between who is Mohawk and who gains status is not exact, nor is the system devised to determine this identity always consistent and/or fair. Furthermore, the possession of status does not equate to an ability to clearly articulate the fundamental characteristics of Mohawk identity, although that identity may not be questioned as a result of its automatic conferral at birth.

Sandra, the child of a Mohawk mother and Euro-Canadian father, was raised and continues to live in her middle age on the Kahnawake Reserve. When she applied for status soon after the creation of the Kahnawake Membership Law in 2004, she was denied with the explanation that one of her four great-grandparents, Ida Paul, who was Mohawk and French, "acted white" and, therefore, for all intents and purposes, *was white* (Deer "Interview"). In response, Sandra states, "She [Ida Paul] was born here, she grew up here, she married a Mohawk man, and they both raised their kids as Mohawks. They immersed themselves in the culture. . . . If that doesn't make her a Mohawk woman, I don't know what does. . . . Blood quantum is the whole basis of the fight that I'm going through today." Sandra explains how the Indian Act has exercised a pervasive influence in her life:

> Here in Kahnawake we have what's called the Mohawk Registry. I was never on it, since the day I was born, because when my mother married my father she lost her rights as a Native as per the Indian Act, which was in effect at the time. I grew up on this reserve, but I wasn't allowed to attend school here. I was bussed off the reserve to school in the neighboring community. To this day, I'm not allowed to vote in our elections; I can't own property; I can't build a house if I chose to; if I die, I won't be able to be buried here, right on Mohawk territory in my own cemetery. I'd probably be shipped to Chateaugay.[16]

Importantly, Sandra draws attention to matrilineal descent as a way of defining identity ("My mother's Native. Doesn't that count for anything?"), traditional knowledge ("We have a clan. We were always told we had a clan"), and birth ("To me, it's just a birthright").

Deer also portrays the application process of Lauren Giles, a woman of half Mohawk and half African American ancestry, who applies for status when she turns eighteen. Lauren explains the racism she experienced as a child growing up in Kahnawake as an expression of self-hate: "There's so much mixture in this town. . . . Nobody is 100 percent any more." Like Sandra, Lauren desires inclusion via membership in the Kahnawake Band of Mohawks: "I want to be able to call it home. I want my opinion to count, and to matter, and to have weight in the community. . . . I want to be able to say I'm from Kahnawake and represent the community." Like Sandra, Lauren also possesses a great-grandmother who was half non-Native amongst her four great-grandparents through her Mohawk mother; however, the Council of Elders accepts her application, after a comparatively long deliberation in contrast to Sandra, while stipulating that they will review her case every two years for the next six years to assess her behavior. Lauren states in *Club Native* that she does not believe in the Membership Law; however, after being provisionally accepted as a band member, she reflects that she will now be careful of whom she dates and that she will uphold the rules of the Kahnawake Membership Law, illustrating the extent to which this system has potential to hegemonically encourage conformity:

> Before, I had no rights here at all, so I'm content with my situation now, and I will do everything in my power not to lose my standing here. But . . . in the future if I meet a nice fella who's not from around here, then— so be it. I understand the consequences of my actions. . . . I think that's [the Membership Law and consequences for choosing a non-Native partner] something that should be respected. . . . These are the laws that we're abiding by now. Even though it's something that I don't agree with, I agreed to go through the process. I signed the papers; I signed the contract.

Despite its emphasis upon blood quantum, being accepted as a community member with full rights, however subject to revision, means something important to Lauren: "I am a member of Kahnawake now . . . , part of the community." Thus, what Deer figures as a birthright to Kahnawake community members *as distinct from status Kahnawake Mohawks*—now transformed into a contract to be signed, not unlike a treaty—still possesses an emotional and epistemic hold on how Lauren imagines her identity.

In contrast, traditional methods of reckoning nation and clan were significantly different from the 2004 Membership Law, as Deer outlines in a narrative segue. As Deer's niece, Kasennonkwas, the oldest child of Tiffany and her non-Native partner Andrew, colors traditional images of longhouse life, the voices of Deer's Speaker's Corner interviewees collaboratively make the following statement:

> The custom . . . has its origins back to Haudenosaunee, which existed for centuries before Columbus, and nowhere in that culture is there any mention of blood. It had nothing to do with blood. It had everything to do with custom, culture, language, sense of belonging. *And the stories were that when the white people came and raided our village and killed our women and children, our Indian men would go and do the same, but they'd take back the children and raise them as Indians. So there's a mixture of blood in here.* Now the law also says when you come into the house you leave behind what you had before. That's gone. You're now part of us. This is how you act, this is what you do. *And our clans meant a lot to us. That's not to say . . . "I'm a wolf, and I'll wear a wolf t-shirt and put a wolf sticker on my car." That's not what a clan is for. Traditionally, it tied people together, and people worked together to ensure that we survived.* We were so accepting of people before. People could be adopted into a clan. *We adopted people whether they were Native or non-Native.* We survived because we have adapted. *Even though we have our family, it was life, you know, living.*[17]

Significantly, the Speaker's Corner commentators do not articulate an investment in matrilineal descent per se, which was the common practice for determining identity prior to contact with Europeans; what is evident in their commentary is that adoption was a community function for transforming an outsider into an insider and useful contributor to village life.[18] This omission of reliance on matrilineal descent seems to both obviate a rigid insistence upon pre-contact traditions that would detribalize many in the Kahnawake Band of Mohawks (who retained status on the basis of patrilineal descent and *lost* status on the basis of matrilineal descent) and destabilizes the internalized assumptions regarding blood quantum inherent in the management of C-31 status Indians via the Membership

21. *Club Native* still. Speaker's Corner interviewee Alex M. McComber. Courtesy of Tracey Penelope Tekahentahkwa Deer.

Law. Significantly, the commentators specifically explain how adoption into the Hodinöhsö:ni' was a common practice *both* before contact and after contact ("when the white people came") and that this method kept populations and families intact and healthy.

In "Mohawks in High Steel," Joseph Mitchell (Mohawk) makes the following observation about the origins of Caughnawaga:

> The Caughnawagas are among the oldest reservation Indians. The band had its origins in the latter half of the seventeenth century, when French Jesuit missionaries converted somewhere between fifty and a hundred Iroquois families in a dozen longhouse villages in what is now western and northern New York and persuaded them to go up to Quebec and settle in a mission outpost. This outpost was on the St. Lawrence, down below Lachine Rapids. The converts began arriving there in 1668. Among them were members of all the tribes in the Iroquois Confederacy—Mohawks, Oneidas, Onondagas, Cayugas, and Senecas. There were also a few Hurons, Eries, and Ottawas who had been captured and adopted by the Iroquois and had been living with them in the longhouse villages. Mohawks greatly predominated, and Mohawk customs and the

22. *Club Native* still. Speaker's Corner interviewee Timmy Norton. Courtesy of Tracey Penelope Tekahentahkwa Deer.

Mohawk dialect of Iroquois eventually became the customs and speech of the whole group.[19]

Mitchell's brief history of the formation of Caughnawaga highlights the community's continued cultural diversity from origins to present *and* the role of adoption as part of a complexly defined, normative identity based on behavior and quality of character instead of blood. The Speaker's Corner interviewees explicate these historically Indigenous methods for determining identity that have obvious pertinence in the present era: "We were so accepting of people before [the Indian Act]"; "We adopted people whether they were Native or non-Native"; "We survived because we have adapted [and adopted, *explication my own*]." Alex McComber articulates that "It's not what your blood is, it's who your family is. The other most important piece is who you are, and how you walk, and how you act, and what you contribute."

A number of interviewees have held and continue to hold prominent roles in the application of the Kahnawake Membership Law, and their commentary on how it performs in reality is very illustrative of the contrast between Indigenous reckoning and blood quantum determinations:

23. *Club Native* still. Speaker's Corner interviewee Tammy Beauvais. Courtesy of Tracey Penelope Tekahentahkwa Deer.

Mike Delisle Jr., Grand Chief of Kahnawake—"People look across the table and say, 'Iahten-Onkwehonwe,' because we know what that means in English: 'they're not Mohawk; they're not Native,' and it's wrong . . . because one of their parents are white or they know that one of their great grandparents didn't come from Kahnawake or whatever their background history is, and that goes on for generations and generations, and I think it's become a real thorn in our society's side."[20]

Watio Montour, former member of the Council of Elders—"I left the Elders Council because I disagreed with the decision. You know, they're basing it on blood, or so it seems. They're saying it's not, but the evidence is clear the four great-grandparent stipulation is basically blood quantum, and that's how we're basing our decision on people's lives, and everything else means nothing—nothing."

Other Speaker's Corner interviewees further develop these insider observations. Kahnawake Mohawk designer Tammy Beauvais contends, "That was the intention of the Indian Act, you know. That was the intention for us to be doing that to each other now." Patty Bush Stacey elaborates, "We have learned well from the non-Native society . . . what do do with our

24. *Club Native* still. Speaker's Corner interviewee Patty Bush Stacey. Courtesy of Tracey Penelope Tekahentahkwa Deer.

own people to separate us." Deidre Diome observes, "If the whole point of Membership was to build up or preserve the cultural identity of the Kahnawake people, I have to say that it has failed." Lauren's mother Carolyn Skye asserts that the "process [itself] goes against tradition."

One of the most noteworthy accomplishments of *Club Native* is the community members' refusal to be silenced by colonial attitudes, although their decisions to speak are obviously mediated by a concern to speak in such a way as to be helpful, not harmful, to their community. Kahnawake Mohawk scholar Audra Simpson has written specifically about "ethnographic refusal" and the choice of silence on the topic of membership in Kahnawake in her essay, "On Ethnographic Refusal: Indigeneity, 'Voice,' and Colonial Citizenship." Reflecting on an interview with an informant who lacks status, owing to his mother's marriage to a non-Native prior to Bill C-31, and who claims "[n]o one seems to know why" his mother has not been reinstated, Simpson observes:

> Everyone knows everyone's "predicament". . . . I won't get into it with my readers. What I am quiet about is his predicament and my predicament and the actual stuff (the math, the clans, the mess, and misrecognitions,

the confusion and the clarity) – the calculus of our predicaments. . . . Can I do this and still come home; what am I revealing here and why? Where will this get us? Who benefits from this and why? And "enough" was when they shut down (or told me to turn off the recorder), or told me outright funny things like "nobody seems to know" – when everybody *does* know and talks about it *all the time.* Dominion had to be exercised over these representations. . . . The ethnographic limit . . . was arrived at when the representation would bite all of us and compromise the *representational* territory that we have gained for ourselves in the past 100 years, in small but deeply influential ways. . . . [21]

Collectively, the community of Kahnawake, or the community of interviewees who choose to speak with Deer in *Club Native*, have decided to expand the limits of their discourse, because the stakes are high enough to merit the risks attendant to representation. This same spectre of refusal is present in *Club Native*, but is overridden by the desire to articulate "'feeling citizenships' that are structured in the present space of intra-community recognition, affection, and care, outside of the logics of colonial and imperial rule."[22]

Deer's documentary analysis of the impact of enforcing the Membership Law on Kahnawake women with non-Native partners focuses on the stories of Waneek Horn-Miller and Deer's sister, Wahsontiiostha Tiffany Deer. Both women have chosen non-Native partners in the face of community disapproval and, in Horn-Miller's case, familial rejection; both women ideally envisioned themselves as partnered to Mohawk men, but chose a better personal match over their own hopes of having a Native partner and status children. Deer is quick to point out that the ramifications for these choices, whether under the Indian Act or post-Bill C-31, are much less severe for Mohawk men who choose to marry out; under the Indian Act, men who married out Indianized their wives, whereas Mohawk women who married non-Natives lost their status and *had to move off-reserve.* Even now, given the high visibility of mixed race children, women's behavior seems to be more closely scrutinized at Kahnawake, and women are under greater threat of being forced to move off-reserve. Vandalism and intimidation have been tools in motivating some Kahnawake women to move off-territory.

In interviews, Waneek talks about suffering from posttraumatic stress disorder (PTSD) post-Oka and post-Olympics and asking Creator to "send" her someone to help her. After trying to find the perfect Native man for years, Horn-Miller met Keith, a fellow Olympian, who turned out to be "that person [she] wished for and hoped for [who happened to] be white." Waneek states that choosing to be with Keith "goes against just about everything I've been brought up with."[23] The turning point for Horn-Miller was when she told Keith "I need to have Native children," and he told her, "Waneek, I will never, ever stop you from doing what you need to do for your people. I just want to be there to help you raise the kids." Horn-Miller's choice to be partnered to a non-Native has "affected my family a lot . . . ; it's created strife. . . . It's kind of hard to know that you're causing that sadness [in the hearts of my family] and those fights. . . . It's just hard to know that you're a disappointment . . . , that our relationship can be seen as a disappointment." Despite her family's rejection, Horn-Miller has chosen to remain in Kahnawake, build a house, and have biological children with Keith, even in the face of vandals writing "Go home, Frenchman!" on the construction site of her house. Choosing to remain in Kahnawake *and* build there in the face of intensifying feelings around status and non-Native partners is a decisive and brave act, one with specific historic resonances: in the 1970s, Kahnawake community members and their non-Native partners were taken from their homes in the middle of the night and dropped at the border of the reserve by other Kahnawake Mohawks.[24] Community members have told Waneek, "You're not Mohawk any more. You're Canadian. Get out of here. You have no right to be here."[25]

Like Waneek, Wahsiontiiostha has also made a decision to remain in Kahnawake to deliver and to raise her children, though she divided time between Kahnawake and Austin while her eldest daughter was not yet in pre-school. Like Waneek, Tiffany reached adulthood thinking that she had to have "the most Native" kid and had to marry a Native. However, these plans were thrown off-kilter when she met Andrew while living at the Rhizome Collective in Texas. Tiffany states that she will fight if she and her family are evicted, "because we belong to this community and she [her daughter Kasennonkwas] belongs here. She deserves to grow up here, too." The current Membership Law disallows not only marriage to a non-Native but "living in a common law relationship whether it's in Kahnawake or anywhere else in the world." Tracey Deer points out that living together is "enough to get my sister kicked off the band list," though the "rules are not being enforced yet."

While Tiffany's offspring will not have membership, but will be subject to applying for membership at age 18 under the current Membership Law, Tiffany has no doubt that her daughters, Kasennonkwas and Teiokwirathe, will have a full grounding in Mohawk culture: "I don't even have a doubt that the baby's not going to have . . . a firm grounding and a firm . . . pride and background . . . [or be a] part of community, part of the people, part of a culture. I just know that." Tiffany also rejects the mechanisms that would disbar her children from membership: "I don't think it's right, that somebody shouldn't be accepted when . . . they're fully dedicated." Like Tiffany, Waneek also uses a litmus separate from blood quantum to think about her children's identity as Mohawks: "I would like for my family to be seen as full participating members of the community whether they're adopted children or biological children. . . . Hopefully, the world will judge them not by the color of their skin, but more the content of their character and what they have in their hearts."[26]

The opinions of American Indian academics who study identity formation in Indigenous communities are similarly fluid while reflective of the conflicted attitudes surrounding marrying out. In *X-Marks: Native Signatures of Assent*, Scott Lyons (Ojibwe/Dakota) recounts a personal occurrence at a powwow where his light-skinned daughter was called a "white girl" by a Native teenage boy who implied that she was non-Native. His daughter replied in Ojibwe, "telling him that she was in fact an Ojibwe girl with a name, a clan, and a nation, and asking if he understood, which he obviously did not." Lyons remains pleased that she "resolved it [this Indian identity controversy] to her benefit."[27] Yet, he relates that his daughter later felt the complexity of what it means to be marked as "a white girl" of Indian descent. Lyons's conclusion seems to be that cultural knowledge trumps blood quantum; yet, community sanction of one's identity is also fundamentally central to claiming Indianness. Leslie Marmon Silko, however, places the burden of identity and one's place in community solely upon behavior (i.e., culture and the community's metric for it), while acknowledging the historical changes in how Pueblos conceptualize race:

> Younger people, people my parents' age, seemed to look at the world in a more modern way. The modern way included racism. My physical appearance [being light-skinned] seemed not to matter to the old-time people. They looked the world very differently; a person's appearance and possessions did not matter nearly as much as a person's behavior. For them, a person's value lies in how that person interacts with other people, how that person behaves toward the animals and the earth. That is what matters most to the old-time people. The Pueblo people believed this long before the Puritans arrived with their notions of sin, damnation, and racism. The old-time beliefs persist today; thus I will refer to the old-time people in the present tense as well as the past. Many worlds may coexist here.[28]

Thus, like Deer's project, Silko claims that traditional ways of reckoning identity may be carried forward into the present and future; they are as pertinent, or perhaps more, in contending with the neocolonial context.

Gail Guthrie Valaskakis (Chippewa) offers some helpful insights into the role of blood in identity formation and membership determination:

> Native solidarity is spliced with blood borders that sometimes spiral between tribes and within communities. This complex of Indian bloodism is prolonged and layered, and it engages issues of cultural, local, and personal identity and tribal membership that both unify and divide Native people. Today, the Native struggle to construct, represent and regulate tribal communities—and expressions of pan-Indianism—as blood-related unities is linked in articulation to tensions that are both historical and current. In North America, *there is an unrelenting perception that Indianness is cultural but that being Indian is racial* [emphasis mine]. Indians may share this perception today, but race has not always been a determining factor in the formation of Indian nations or tribal communities.[29]

Valaskakis' differentiation between "Indianness" and "being Indian" points to tensions between traditional reckonings of identity and absorbed (originally) non-Indian theories of race. Like Deer and others, Valaskakis acknowledges the pre-contact presence of "tribally hybrid societies" that practiced proximal cohabitation, adoption, and intermarriage.

In *Real Indians: Identity and the Survival of Native America*, Eva Marie Garroutte, an enrolled Cherokee citizen and sociologist, sets out to provide "Indian communities new ways to respond to identity issues with the seriousness they merit yet without being destroyed by the increasingly acrimonious arguments that surround them."[30] Garroutte's analysis begins with recognizing a category of Indians referred to as "outalucks," using esteemed Choctaw/Cherokee novelist Louis Owens as a primary example. Like Sandra, outalucks lack the means "to negotiate their identity as Indians within the available legal definitions;"[31] for Sandra, these restrictions are posed by the application of the Kahnawake Membership Law, not the law itself. Garroutte notes that inability to gain legal standing as an Indian is caused by fractionated blood quantum (within one tribe or within multiple tribes), incorrect descent (reckoned through the wrong parent), and other strictures upon how identity is determined (i.e., presence of ancestors on base rolls, death of an ancestor while base rolls were produced).

Like Deer, Garroutte raises adoption as a method for converting non-Indian status to Indian status. She cites the example of the Keeweenaw Bay Indian Community, which disenrolled two hundred tribal citizens after a tribal election and later adopted these former members back into the Nation, though they no longer held the right to vote in tribal elections as a result of their adopted status. As a second example, Garroutte discusses country western singer Shania Twain who is an enrolled member of the Temagami Bear Island First Nation by virtue of her step-father's full-blood status; Twain apparently lacks any blood descent from tribal nations through either of her biological parents. Yet, Twain strongly culturally identifies with her Native American upbringing and has won an award from First Americans in the Arts. The protest over Twain's presumed Indian identity highlights the entwinement of blood quantum with Indianness within and without Native communities, according to Garroutte.[32] Biological definitions of racial identity have their roots in nineteenth and twentieth-century non-Native racial theories, and they lead to internalized conclusions that full bloods are "really real" while those with lower blood quantum are progressively less authentic.[33]

Regarding internalized trauma surrounding definitions of Indian identity, Eva Marie Garroutte writes, "Anxieties about identity have stifled useful discussion on a variety of subjects by creating an aura of suspicion and even rage."[34] Tracey Deer's *Club Native* portrays a First Nations community teetering dangerously on the brink of such a breakdown in communication. Thankfully, recent community meetings (2010) on the topic of the Membership Law have productively resulted in a greater mutual understanding in the community and a temporary suspension of the Elders Council until satisfactory resolution of the Membership Law controversy has been reached.[35] Meanwhile, Garroutte proposes an approach of "Radical Indigenism" for communities seeking to define their enrollment or status in keeping with tribal epistemologies:

> Is there a way for Indian people to move beyond the divisive animosity of intense conflicts over identity? I believe that there is. I also believe that there is a way to bring together the project of Indian people to live together in communities in a good way *with* the project of the academy to cultivate knowledge. . . . Radical Indigenism illuminates differences in assumptions about knowledge that are at the root of the dominant culture's misunderstanding and subordination of indigenous knowledge. It argues for the reassertion and rebuilding of traditional knowledge from its roots, its fundamental principles.[36]

My interpretation of Tracey Deer's body of filmic work as a communal reading the Adoption Belt fall in line with Garroutte's prescription for advancing Indigenous knowledges as defining principles in reckoning membership. Moreover, Garroutte's statement highlights how Deer's efforts are centered on community healing and recovery as well as preventing further damage to the coming generations.[37] As Deer implores, "We need to start talking about the things that are tearing us apart, and we need to ask political questions. But they need to be asked in a human context. We're all the same people."[38] I would argue that Deer has been tremendously successful in positing these humane questions in her documentary *Club Native*; furthermore, she has facilitated community members speaking through her film and collectively reading the wampum, in this case, the Adoption Belt. At the same time, Deer does not simply "resurrect[] old laws and structures," a strategy that Taiaiake Alfred cautions against in *Wasáse: Indigenous Pathways of Action and Freedom*. Instead, Deer, engages in "the regeneration of Onkwehonwe existences free from colonial attitudes and behaviors." As Alfred suggests, the community of Kahnawake:ronon who speak in *Club Native*

> [s]elf-consciously recreate[s] our cultural practices and reform[s] our political identities by drawing on tradition in a thoughtful process of reconstruction and a committed reorganization of our lives in a personal and collective sense. This will result in a new sense of what it means to live as Onkwehonwe.[39]

The community gathering of traditional knowledge in *Club Native* serves to bring Kahnawake Mohawk cultural ideals into the present, while inflecting and transforming them for changed conditions of Indigenous existence, and it ensures the continued use of these renewed traditions in the future for the purposes of building community.

5

Conclusion

Wampum and the Future of
Hodinöhsö:ni' Narrative Epistemology

Wampum belts carry knowledges that have implications and applications that are far reaching, touching upon topics as germane as cultural integrity and transmission, sovereignty and self-determination, and subjects as contentious as treaty rights and their assertions in manifold contemporary contexts. In this study, I have sought to establish the narrative complexity and significance of wampum to the cultural survival, intellectual transmission, and narrative representation of Hodinöhsö:ni' peoples. The narratives held in wampum belts and the efforts of those Hodinöhsö:ni' intellectuals who reclaim, innovate, and comment upon them clearly have significance for the stories that comprise our day-to-day existence. Further, the fact that each artist and author works in seeming isolation, yet is continually engaged in a larger conversation about Iroquois knowledge and traditions illustrates that the ramifications of their work lies well beyond the bounds of this study and suggests that the scope of wampum's cross-fertilization extends far into the scholarly and aesthetic realm.

These artists form a movement of Hodinöhsö:ni' culture workers who have picked up anew a form that has had tremendous prescience and relevance for Hodinöhsö:ni' peoples for hundreds of years, and despite the fact they have encountered these materials in isolation from each other, they have found the wampum form of vital significance to their rendering of visual and print narratives and have incorporated the form into expressive artistic works in their own unique ways. The manner of each adaptation, innovation, and rearticulation of the wampum strings and belts tells us something important about the adaptability and potency of wampum as a record of Indigenous thought and its capacity to re-center conversations long after the original wampum maker has departed. These artists have happened upon former conversations faithfully recorded in the wampum belts, begun a conversation with that holder, and found ways to string those knowledges into the warp and weft of their own expressive rendition, which incorporates the belt's retelling. Were these records, such as those by Gansworth, Niro, Deer, and Stevens, considered today as works of art and literature, to sit unattended for years, the larger knowledge of wampum circulating in Hodinöhsö:ni' communities would allow a new Ögwe'öweh wampum reader to pick the works up, read them, and find new applications for these narratives in her own existence.[1] Simultaneously, I would refuse any notion of a singular authentic reading of each of these belts, as each author and artist I have considered creates a new wampum narrative that often supersedes the original forms of the wampum belt where they exist and sometimes renders entirely new wampum patterns (i.e., Gansworth, Niro).

James Thomas Stevens takes up the Two Row Wampum, a foundational belt in Hodinöhsö:ni'-European relations, and finds complex new ways to interweave the visual form of the Two Row and its philosophy of international relations into contemporary experimental poetry. His rendering of the Two Row Wampum and the muddy territories of colonialist rhetorics performs the struggle to disentangle oneself from non-Native ways of knowing while simultaneously recognizing the impossibility of complete separation from settler attitudes and culture; Stevens personally acknowledges his recognition and honoring of both his Hodinöhsö:ni' and non-Native ancestry, as his work exemplifies the impossibility of complete separation. For Stevens, the Two Row becomes a method for dramatizing the situation of the Fourth-World citizen, colonized from without and from within, sometimes complicit and always entwined in settler/Native power struggles, and Stevens models an intellectual process for negotiating those complexities that emanates from Two Row teachings.

Friendship chains are emblems of wampum communiqués in the popular imagination, and the relationship of friendship and amity that they signal is pivotal to all treaty relations. Eric Gansworth works continually with friendship chains throughout his fiction, poetry, and paintings, and in *Smoke Dancing* he places print and acrylic in creative dialogue, matching the spoken word of the treaty with the wampum's visual code. Central to this performative reading of the wampum is the Canandaigua Treaty Belt, a friendship belt that records agreements made between Americans and the Six Nations in 1794 and which is the litmus test for many sovereign claims within the boundaries of what is now New York State. Gansworth's depictions of the Canandaigua Treaty Belt send intermittent wampum code transmissions to the viewer that shape each reading based upon the context in which the belt is presented, and the novel's central conflict between tobacco and gasoline entrepreneurs and traditional leadership enacts a discursive tension present between competing contemporary readings of the Canandaigua Treaty Belt. Gansworth's paintings and narratives provide us with an aesthetic exploration of the significations of this treaty belt and a treaty-based methodology for critiquing the settler government's international diplomacy vis-à-vis the Six Nations and other Indigenous nations of North America; Gansworth contributes a fully formed intellectual methodology for applying treaty belts to colonial encounters and recentering narratives of empire and acquisition; his intellectual frame takes a prominent role in Iroquois conversations about wampum, both in this study and without, inspiring the discussants and originators of Hodinöhsö:ni' knowledges in the present and in the future. In short, Gansworth's opus of print and visual art and its focus on wampum belts promises to shape the intellectual continuance and revitalization of Hodinöhsö:ni' epistemic practices and narrative for generations moving forward, particularly in light of his adaptation of wampum to contemporary and pop cultural forms, themes, and compositional structures.

Shelley Niro infuses much of her work with wampum imagery across multiple media, engaging varied artistic forms in a fashion similar to Gansworth; her wampum images occur in beadwork, photography, film, painting, sculpture, and multimedia installations. Her recursive taking up of the wampum beads and string and her creative incorporation of the medium into her artistic endeavors point to wampum's centrality to Hodinöhsö:ni' intellectual practices. Niro's portrayal of wampum in

Kissed by Lightning guides her viewers into reflection upon its origins in condolence and the Great Law of Peace and possible applications of these traditional teachings in day-to-day struggles. By repositioning the Mother of Nations as central to the Great Law and the power of wampum, and thereby condolence, Niro performs a rematriation of the Mother of Nations within the Hodinöhsö:ni' visual, oral, and print traditions. Further, this reclamation provides a model for Red Feminist creative and intellectual endeavors that will allow for a rebalancing and healing of relationships and families within Indian Country, a recovery rooted in Hodinöhsö:ni' gender traditions that uses Indigenous methods of healing and reconciliation for its successful recuperation.

Like Niro, Tracey Deer addresses the position of women in Hodinöhsö:ni' communities and their embattled position(s) under colonialism in her filmmaking, and Deer directs her use of documentary to analyze the impact of the Indian Act on Indigenous self-governance and the status of women within her home community of Kahnawake. Because of the interruption posed by the Indian Act to band membership and by similar policies of enfranchisement to Indigenous traditional governments, an intervention of the kind performed by Deer's *Club Native* makes clarifying (and public) engagements of the issues underpinning Kahnawake women's unique status vis-à-vis enrollment possible.[2] In this film, Deer's community collectively reads the Adoption Belt as a way of recuperating women's roles in determining community membership, intervening in internalized colonialist practices that serve to disempower women, *and* creatively responding to the ways in which settler blood quantum laws have fractionated Indian identity and fractured Indian communities. Like Gansworth, Deer's documentary narrative gestures toward the wisdom held in wampum and the epistemes within that may be unlocked to trigger ancestral memory and recover the Indigenous ability to heal and continue.

As I have illustrated, the pragmatic orientation of works by Gansworth and Deer make specific, material, and localized contributions to larger decolonization movements and to the further affirmation and development of Hodinöhsö:ni' cultural traditions. The works of all of the artists considered in this study reinforce existing bodies of knowledge associated with wampum belts and innovate them in important ways that allow for regeneration of existing knowledges and production of new epistemic practices that are uniquely Hodinöhsö:ni'. The study of these works, and similar works by other Iroquois artists, defines a trajectory of Hodinöhsö:ni' cultural resurgence and vital intellectual traditions that furnish a path for the coming generations to follow in their own artistic and legal development and production.

The works studied herein illustrate how wampum traditions and teachings continue to have political and cultural applications in contemporary settings. These print and visual works have a pragmatic impact in their recounting and reaffirmation of traditions that are tribally specific *and* pertinent to the international policy formation of the United States and Canada. That wampum has a pivotal role in the Condolence Ceremony and the raising up of chiefs (and the knowledge they represent) has inestimable significance for the acts of narrative rearticulation and knowledge recovery via reclamation and reapplication in new contexts created by this new generation of strategists for survival. These artists' intellectual and aesthetic endeavors affirm wampum's role as a touchstone of Iroquois experience and ways of being that is continually adaptable to new settings and historical eras and that the knowledge it carries always has the potential to be requickened, in spite of colonialist projects to squelch its powers.

There was a time in the twentieth century when nearly all wampum belts had been "acquired" or stolen by museums and individual collectors, and very few Hodinöhsö:ni' youth or adults had the benefit of accessing wampum as part of a shared cultural tradition, as part of their expression of being uniquely Iroquois. As at other times of great difficulty in Hodinöhsö:ni' history, individuals arose to right the existing imbalance; in the case of wampum, Tehanetorens Ray Fadden came to play a unique role in the revitalization of wampum and larger Iroquois cultural and ceremonial traditions.

Starting in the 1930s, Ray Fadden worked as a schoolteacher at the Tuscarora Reservation in Lewiston, New York. Influenced by legendary Tuscarora activist Clinton Rickard, Fadden cultivated a sense of cultural pride amongst his students that they carried forward into their daily lives. In the 1950s, Fadden, a non-Native, relocated with his Mohawk wife Christina, to the Akwesasne Mohawk Reserve. As at Lewiston with the Tuscaroras, Fadden was instrumental in teaching Akwesasne Mohawk children their cultural traditions and instilling a sense of ethnic pride. He also began research on wampum traditions, using the belts as teaching tools at the Akwesasne Freedom School, and was eventually adopted into the Akwesasne Band of Mohawks. Over a number of years, Fadden interviewed numerous elders at Akwesasne on the use of wampum, and he created replicas of wampum belts that were later housed in the Six Nations Indian Museum, which he established in 1954 and ran in his retirement. He published a landmark study of wampum, *Wampum Belts of the Iroquois*, which featured photographs of his Mohawk students holding many of the belts and individual histories for each belt.[3]

Fadden taught as children or engaged as adults a large population of community leaders at Akwesasne and at the Six Nations Indian Museum, including Tom Porter, Doug George, Kay Olan, Maurice Kenny, and many others, and the transfer of his museum collection to the Hiawatha Institute for Indigenous Knowledge ensures his life's work on wampum and longhouse culture will be carried forward to coming generations. Some of Fadden's most prescient writing and curation centered upon wampum, from his earliest publications to his later works, confirming wampum's vital role in transmitting Hodinöhsö:ni' knowledge, narrative, and models for community.

The teachings of Tehanetorens have had long-reaching effects. For instance, the many children photographed holding wampum belts in *Wampum Belts of the Iroquois* were part of a cultural revitalization movement that brought the longhouse religion back to Akwesasne. That longhouse has in turn been a locus of political action, including reoccupying unceded Mohawk Territory since the 1960s. More recently, a group of men representing the Men's Council of the People of the Way of the Longhouse reoccupied a 240-acre parcel of land currently deeded to non-Native Horst Wuerching on March 2, 2009. Kaneretiio William Roger Jock, who was a young teenager when he was photographed holding the Huron Alliance Belt, Great Britain and Six Nations Friendship Belt, and the Confessional Wampum of Handsome Lake, is now being charged by the county authorities with second degree grand larceny for stealing this land. Jock asserts, "We're only reclaiming what is ours" under the 1797 Seven Nations Treaty, which set aside the Hogansburg Triangle for the Akwesasne Mohawks.[4] This treaty requires the consent of Congress for any further amendments to it, but while New York State did enter into six subsequent treaties with the St. Regis Mohawks, Congress did not ratify these treaties, thus nullifying them under the Indian Trade and Intercourse Act of 1790, and that act's subsequent expansion under the broader Nonintercourse Act.

This case stands to overturn existing centuries of court decisions on the New York land claims, and it also illustrates the power of wampum as records of international diplomacy. By occupying their sovereign territories, as vouchsafed in numerous treaties, the Men's Council of Akwesasne, in effect, reclaims Hodinöhsö:ni' intellectual traditions and affirms their own control of Indigenous narrative and self-representation. In the most pragmatic sense, the Men's Council is claiming the inheritance and the future of all Akwesasne Mohawks and the larger Six Nations and Seven Nations alliances of which they are a part. Similarly, by claiming, reframing, and rearticulating wampum images in their works, Stevens, Gansworth, Niro, and Deer breathe life again into the wampum traditions: they do not simply allude to them as signifiers of a bygone tradition; they remake and add to that tradition by showing the ways in which wampum teachings are still relevant to the challenges faced by Hodinöhsö:ni' peoples in the present.

Through my study of these artists' wampum narratives, wampum in its many forms emerges as a living tradition, one that has a purchase on the minds of Hodinöhsö:ni' peoples in the present and the relationships between Hodinöhsö:ni' peoples and settler governments. In this reclamation of wampum lies the potential to give birth to a revivified and strengthened Hodinöhsö:ni' intellectualism, one that supports and heals the nations and that provides a capacious repertoire for engaging settler institutions and policies with inestimable critical potency. Further, beyond a rhetoric of equivalences (nation to nation, sovereign to sovereign), wampum narratives in shell, print, film, and other media carry knowledges capable of adaptations and permutations that exceed the known possibilities of Eurowestern print narratives. Through the joining of mnemonic practices and numerous media, contemporary wampum narratives pull from the repository of knowledge and energy formed by the original wampum belts, wampum creation, and wampum readings, and they grow further through the addition of the new forms, which place differing demands on the means of wampum's expression. Further, the wampum forms transform the new media in which they are represented, presenting new expressive methods and strategies through wampum's symbolic and narrative functions. The authors, artists, and filmmakers discussed in this study form a new discursive longhouse in which wampum belts are created with specific intent in local contexts and, additionally, are brought to a larger audience beyond the longhouse for their engagements. These new wampum belts pull from old knowledges, requicken those knowledges, and amend growing wisdom to contemporary glosses of those traditions; further, these artists also innovate and create new traditions that speak to the contemporary moment and to the future in a distinctively Iroquois way. Their actions bring new insights to the coming generations and form a unique community of wampum creators and readers, furthering the continuance of Hodinöhsö:ni' epistemic and aesthetic practices.

Notes ⊞ *Bibliography* ⊞ *Index*

Notes

Introduction: Hodinöhsö:ni' Visual Code and Intellectual Transmission

1. Rice, *Kwah Í:ken Tsi Iroquois*, 59.

2. Keating, *Iroquois Art*, 3.

3. Ted Williams recounts the history of Hodinöhsö:ni' spiritual practices moving from the public to the private realm: "At the time of the burning of witches at Salem, the great seers among the indigenous peoples of the eastern United States immediately 'saw' this event, and all ceremony, also referred to as Medicine activity, went underground. . . . So if white people were unacquainted with Indian Medicine ways before this, then it became nearly impossible to ever discover the depth of those Medicine ways. Whether the seers sounded an all-clear or not, some of the Six Nations people gradually began practicing more openly." Williams, *Big Medicine*, 27. I cite Williams here to illustrate that spiritual matters have not always necessitated protection from unbelieving outsiders: "Disbelief dilutes any Medicine to the degree of the disbelief." Ibid., 29.

4. It is worth noting that Tenskwatawa, the Shawnee prophet, made wampum belts that were composed of beans or seeds strung on cord. They, too, possessed ritual and political significance and were tied to the political resurgence movement that sometimes operated with the title of the "United Tribal Nations" and included members of Shawnee, Seneca, Potawatomi, Miami, Hurons, Delawares, Ottawas, Cherokees, and Anishinaabeg. Ashbel Woodward notes the Iroquois name for freshwater wampum was *otékoa*. Woodward, *Wampum*, 14. Eileen Phyllis Williams Bardeau uses the term *oyë:ë'* for a single wampum bead. Bardeau, *Definitive Seneca*, 417.

5. Welburn, *Roanoke and Wampum*, xv.

6. Wallace, *White Roots of Peace*, 51–52. Hiawatha is an Iroquois culture hero who helped the Peacemaker spread the message of peace and power throughout the Five Nations in roughly 1142 CE. The more familiar Hiawatha originates in Longfellow's "The Song of Hiawatha," which has been adapted for the stage and is performed each year at Pipestone, Minnesota. For a comprehensive study of the role of these performances of Longfellow's Hiawatha in the creation of American identity, see Alan Trachtenberg's *Shades of Hiawatha*.

7. For descriptions of the four epochs of Hodinöhsö:ni' history, see Barbara Alice Mann, *Iroquoian Women: The Gantowisas*, 32–39 and 49–57.

8. Under duress in 1898, a group of Onondagas designated the Regents of the University of New York temporary wampum keepers, in an effort to curtail illegal thefts of wampum belts which plagued the Confederacy. The following year the New York state legislature signed into law section 27 of the New York State Indian Law, which the university claimed placed "all wampums . . . under its authority. . . . Ironically, the University of the State of New York later decided to bequeath the wampum it had collected to the New York State Museum, rather than return it to the Onondaga." R. Hill, "Regenerating Identity," 135.

9. Muller, "Two 'Mystery' Belts," 129–64. While Muller performs some detailed examination of archival records in her article, she fails to truly substantiate the claim she makes regarding the Two Row Wampum and Two Road Wampum. In fact, she seems to reach a conclusion that favors written records over oral records, which would seem to contradict the very endeavor to research wampum belts; furthermore, her conclusion rests overwhelmingly on the report of one individual, T. R. Roddy, whom historical record has established as a thief and colluder with individuals who had lost the sanction of the traditional chiefs at Six Nations.

10. Richard W. Hill Sr. makes the following observation about rematriation efforts: "The old wampums, descended from the time of the founding of the Iroquois Confederacy, symbolized the ongoing power of the Council of Chiefs. Many modern-day Iroquois believe that the removal of the wampum that ensued was an attempt to destroy the traditional form of government." R. Hill, "Regenerating Identity," 133.

11. Krehbiehl observes that wampum belts "were always a temptation to white men who had none of the scruples of the Indians." Further, he notes that a number of the stolen belts reappeared ("have turned up") in the collections of the New York State Museum and the Smithsonian Association. Krehbiehl, "Iroquois Wampum," 9.

12. Ibid. Hale may have been correct insofar as individual beads or strings comprising belts were of newer fabrication, given that belts were and still are repaired from time to time when they show wear.

13. Ibid., 9.

14. Ibid.

15. Fenton, "Return," 392.

16. The collection and retention of wampum belts that belong to the Confederacy by individual "collectors" is truly egregious, given that they constitute Hodinöhsö:ni' cultural patrimony. In light of American and Canadian settler agendas to eradicate Hodinöhsö:ni' language, culture, and lifeways, the holding hostage of these belts by governments, museums, and individual collectors embodies crimes against humanity and violations of the United Nations Declaration on the Rights of Indigenous Peoples by the US and Canadian governments as signatories of this UN document.

17. Haas, "Wampum as Hypertext," 89 and 92.

18. Ironically, Sally Roesch Wagner clearly establishes that the First Wave feminists of Seneca Falls took their inspiration from Hodinöhsö:ni' women and clanmothers. Wagner, *Sisters in Spirit.*

19. Huhndorf and Suzack, "Indigenous Feminism," 2 and 6.

20. Like the Peacemaker, Seneca tradition states that one should not say the Mother of Nations' name aloud, and it should not appear in print.

21. See McClintock, *Imperial Leather* for more information on the settler colonial studies.

22. As a Seneca-descent individual, I situate my readings in a Hodinöhsö:ni' discursive and scholarly field that privileges Hodinöhsö:ni' scholarship and artistry, and my hope is that by so doing I will highlight the wisdom and insight provided by these artists and authors to Hodinöhsö:ni' and non-Hodinöhsö:ni', Native and non-Native audiences.

23. Leslie Marmon Silko makes the following observation about language growth over the next half millennium:

> In the keynote address I gave to the American Indian Language Development Convention in Tucson in mid-June of 2007 I decided to look into the future to see what languages people here will speak five hundred years from now, and I realized everyone in the Southwest will speak Nahuatl, no Chinese, although Chinese will be the dominant language of finance and commerce world-wise, and everyone's second language. I won't go into the details of the decline of the English language here for lack of space.
>
> The resurgence of Nahuatl will arise out of the sheer numbers of speakers especially in Mexico City, with the largest population of Nahua speakers in the world. Of course a great many of the Indigenous tribal languages of the Americas are related to Nahuatl so I include them as well. (Silko, *Turquoise Ledge*, 40)

24. See *We Still Live Here: Âs Nutayuneân*, directed by Anne Makepeace, for the story of Jessie Little Doe Baird's work to help her community bring back the Wampanoag language.

1. Two Row Wampum in James Thomas Stevens's *A Bridge Dead in the Water* and *Tokinish*

1. Martin-Hill, *Sewatokwa'tshera't*.

2. The Two Row Wampum is commonly referred to as the *Gaswënta'*; however, this term is also broadly applied to all wampum belts.

3. In "Indian Self-Government in the Haudenosaunee Constitution," Oren Lyons identifies the year of the Two Row Wampum's ratification as 1613. 55 *Nordic Journal International* (1986): 119. See Susan Kalter's *Benjamin Franklin, Pennsylvania, and the First Nations: The Treaties of 1736–62* for examples of the Two Row Wampum as the premise for subsequent treaties recorded in the eighteenth century. In their histories and journals, Cadwallader Colden and Conrad Weiser also furnish numerous examples of the recitation of the Two Row at the beginning of treaty proceedings between Hodinöhsö:ni' and Europeans.

4. Oren Lyons, "Indian Self-Government," 119.

5. Jemison, "Sovereignty," 149.

6. Oren Lyons, "Indian Self-Government," 119.

7. See Harmen Meyndertsz van den Bogaert's *A Journey into Mohawk and Oneida Country* for more details.

8. Venables, *Enduring Legacies*, 76. Robert Venables notes of the Treaty of Canandaigua (1794): "Regarding sovereignty, what did the Haudenosaunee expect as a result of the 1794 Treaty of Canandaigua? Speculation is exactly that, especially from this Anglo-American author. In all probability, because the Haudenosaunee viewed treaties as part of a diplomatic continuum, the Treaty of Canandaigua would have been an extension of the premise of the 'Guswenta' or 'Two Row Wampum Belt.' . . . Symbolically, the primary elements of the Guswenta are two parallel rows made of purple wampum, separated by three rows of white wampum." Ibid., citing Jemison and Schein, *Treaty of Canandaigua*, 22–24, 36, and 69–70.

9. Williams and Nelson, "Kaswentha."

10. Williams and Nelson write, "By the twentieth century, the record shows that Canadian government authorities had no personal memory or knowledge of the treaties and promises that had been made and deliberately had no will to find out about them." Ibid. Meanwhile, the importance of the Two Row in Hodinöhsö:ni' memory has not diminished in the slightest: Oren Lyons writes, "We've always taken the position that you must maintain your separate identity and your own identity to protect treaties and land. From the beginning, with our discussion with the Dutch in 1613, we established a treaty called the Two Row Wampum, the Guswenta. We said at that time, 'You will know us by the way we dress.' We take that literally. So today, you'll know us by the way we dress, and that is to clarify our identity." About the extension of citizenship to Native Americans in 1924, Lyons elaborates further: "Knowing that we had a treaty, we understood that when you have an agreement between nations and you obfuscate your national identity, there's going to come a point in time when you're not going to be sure which side of the line you *are* on. If you were an American citizen, it just seemed elementary to us that you could not have a treaty with yourself." Oren Lyons, "Canandaigua Treaty," 70 and 72.

11. Williams and Nelson place the original treaty with the Dutch in 1613, and the British continuation of the treaty in 1664.

12. Williams and Nelson, "Kaswentha."

13. The Six Nations' occupation of the Caledonia site began in 2006 in protest of further development of the Haldimand Tract, which is land originally guaranteed the Six Nations of Grand River under treaty negotiations conducted by Joseph Brant at the close of the American Revolution. A corrupt treaty in 1841, which was protested by Six Nations confederacy chiefs, fractured the band's land holdings and is still contested by the Six Nations to this day. The site has more recently been referred to as Kanonhstaton, but its traditional name is Ohswéken. Dawn Martin-Hill, a Mohawk academic, has directed three documentaries about the basis in treaties and wampum records for the Caledonia land claim: *Jidwá: doh: Let's Become Again* (2005), *Okwànistenhsera: Mothers of Our Nations* (2006), and *Sewatokwa'tshera't: The Dish with One Spoon* (2008).

14. Throughout this essay, I will use the terms "Two Spirit" and "LGBTQ2" (encompassing lesbian, gay, bisexual, transgender, queer, and questioning communities) because of the ability to critique colonial encounters via a queer Indigenous framework, which these terms facilitate. I need to be clear, however, that James Thomas Stevens himself does not identify with the Two Spirit label. James Thomas Stevens, personal communication, February 13, 2011. "(dis)Orientation" is an expression used by Stevens that I argue encompasses a theoretical strategy and poetic praxis for upending colonial assumptions through disorienting settler cartographies and, consequently, also disempowering the normative heteropatriarchal gaze. Stevens's poetry depicts this heteronormative and colonialist gaze as expressly originating in the authors of Jesuit *Relations*, Williams's *Key*, and other early authors of European colonial writings.

15. Gilbert, review of *A Bridge Dead in the Water*.

16. In fact, Two Spirit is the English translation of an Anishinaabe third gender tradition, so it is tribally specific, although it has been generalized for its activist potential to refer to all LGBTQ2 Native American individuals.

17. Driskill, Finley, Gilley, and Morgensen, "Introduction," 3 and 14.

18. Stevens, *A Bridge*, "Introduction."

19. Driskill, Finley, Gilley, and Morgensen, "Introduction," 19.

20. I invoke "decolonial" here in the spirit of Emma Pérez's work on the decolonial imaginary. Pérez defines the decolonial imaginary as "a tool [in Chicana/o history] for uncovering the hidden voices of Chicanas that have been relegated to silences, to passivity, to that third space where agency is enacted through third space feminism." *The Decolonial Imaginary*, xvi. Like Pérez, I imagine the decolonial as a mode in which we may recover lost voices of marginalized Indigenous peoples and bring their voices to the fore of our academic work.

21. Rifkin, *When Did Indians*, 17 and 37.

22. In *Talking Back: Thinking Feminist, Thinking Black*, bell hooks (5) categorizes "talking back" as "speaking as an equal to an authority figure" and "daring to disagree and sometimes . . . just having an opinion." hooks' reclaiming of the pejorative "back talk" is rooted in her rhetorical and literary mentor, her grandmother Bell Hooks, who would often be alluded to when Gloria Watkins was criticized as a child for indulging in "talking back." That bell hooks was a Black Indian and carrier of North American Indigenous oral traditions in Watkins' family should not be overlooked, and I cite her work here as part of claiming hooks and other black Indian scholars within Native American Studies.

23. Stevens, *A Bridge*, 4, lines 61–64.

24. Ibid., 19, lines 292–95. Stevens here alludes to the naming of the town of Lachine, Quebec by explorer Robert Cavelier de la Salle, who was under the mistaken impression that he had reached Asia.

25. Pearce and Louis, "Mapping," 110–11.

26. Johnson, Louis, and Promano, "Facing the Future," 82. Kelley and Francis are quoted in Pearce and Louis, "Mapping," 109.

27. Tonawanda Seneca scholar Mishuana Goeman observes that Native people "must . . . begin to scrutinize the impact of spatial policies in our cognitive mapping of Native lands and bodies. . . . How do we uproot settler maps that drive our everyday materiality and realities?" The implication of Stevens' poetry seems to be that wampum belts perform as the normative map from which to formulate and deploy Iroquois cartographies. Goeman, "Notes," 170.

28. Stevens, *A Bridge*, 7, lines 120–21, and 5, lines 81–83.

29. Stevens, *Combing*, 71, lines 10–11 and 16–18.

30. Stevens, *A Bridge*, 19, lines 274–87.

31. Jacques Marquette departed for New France in 1666 as a Jesuit and died there in 1673. Joseph Henrie Marie de Prémare worked as a missionary in China from 1698 to 1724.

32. Stevens, *A Bridge*, 6, lines 99–107.

33. Ibid., 11, lines 167–68. These words are echoed in Stevens' earlier poem *Tokinish*: "There is a space between your torso and mine, where travel goes. The charting of my course is instinctual but I give destination no name, as the name for you lacks more than its symbol. You are an island or the name of an island. . . . Your body doesn't wait for a name, because it has one in the circumference of my arms, where only the skin can speak it." Stevens, *Combing*, 139.

34. Stevens, *A Bridge*, 10, lines 145–52.

35. Ibid., 14, lines 217–22.

36. Ibid., 21, lines 7–9.

37. Ibid., 21, line 15; 22, line 6; and 23, line 33.

38. Ibid., 24, lines 6–7.

39. Ibid., 24, lines 1–4.

40. Ibid., 27, lines 7–9.

41. Ibid., 28, lines 29–30.

42. Ibid., 28, lines 14–16.

43. Dowling, "Through Its Naming," 191–92 and 204.

44. Stevens, "Poetry and Sexuality," 183.

45. Stevens, *A Bridge*, 39, lines 2–3 and 23–24.

46. Ibid., 40, lines 11–20; 46, lines 1–3; 39, line 26; 42, line 7; and 43, line 18.

47. Ibid., 48, lines 1–3 and 16–18.

48. Ibid., 60, lines 1–24.

49. Stevens alludes here to Tehanetorens Ray Fadden's "Why We Have Mosquitoes" in *Legends of the Iroquois*. Tehanetorens' wife, Christina Fadden, was an adoptive grandmother to James Thomas Stevens' mother. Tehanetorens writes,

> The old Iroquois Indians used to tell this story to the children: Many winters
> in the past two giant mosquitoes appeared on either side of a river. These giant
> creatures were as tall as a good-sized pine tree. As the Indian people paddled

down the river in their canoes, these giant creatures would bend their heads and attack them with their giant beaks. The mosquitoes killed many people. Knowing that these giant mosquitoes were waiting to attack any canoe that floated down the river, the people began to shun that particular stream. It was then that these giant creatures moved to other streams to seek their prey. For a time, it was a reign of terror for the Iroquois who were great canoe travelers. They never knew just when these giant mosquitoes would pounce upon and devour them. Finally, in desperation, a war party was organized to seek out these creatures and destroy them. Twenty warriors in two great canoes floated down a river where they expected the mosquitoes to be. In their hands, ever ready, they held their bow and arrows. Fastened to their belts were their war clubs and hunting knives. Suddenly, two huge shadows loomed over them and a giant beak pierced one of the canoes. Giving their war cry, the warriors filled the air with many arrows. The battle was terrific! The giant mosquitoes seemed to be everywhere at the same time. In a little while half of the warriors had been killed. The remaining braves determined to die courageously. Singing their Death Song, they attacked the huge creatures on land. They hid behind trees and bushes. They surrounded the mosquitoes, who were unable to get at them because of the thick branches. The Iroquois buried many of their arrows in the bodies of the two mosquitoes. Finally, after most of the arrows had been shot and the supply was very low, the two mosquitoes fell to the earth, covered with many wounds. Immediately, the warriors fell upon them with their war clubs and, with powerful blows, tore their bodies apart. From the blood of the two big mosquitoes there sprang many little mosquitoes, and the air was filled with them. These little mosquitoes, like their grandfathers, are fond of the taste of human blood. They hate man for killing their grandfathers and are continually trying to get revenge upon man for this reason.

Fadden, *Legends*, 85–89. A version of "The Great Mosquito" is also included in William Canfield's *Legends of the Iroquois Told by "The Cornplanter,"* 59–61.

50. Stevens, *A Bridge*, 61, lines 31–33.

51. Ibid., 65, lines 5–6, 17–18, and 3–4.

52. Stevens, *Combing*, 142.

53. Dowling, "And Through Its Naming" 196.

54. Stevens, e-mail correspondence with author, November 22, 2010.

55. Stevens, *A Bridge*, 86, lines 11–14.

56. Ibid., 88, lines 1–6 and 11–14.

57. Ibid., 89, lines 3–4.

58. Ibid., 90, lines 4–5; 103, lines 1–14.

59. Ibid., 104.

60. Ibid., 106–7.

61. Williams and Nelson, "Kaswentha."

62. Ibid.

2. The Covenant Chain in Eric Gansworth's Fiction, Poetry, Memoir, and Paintings: The Canandaigua Treaty Belt as Critical Indigenous Economic Critique

1. Mohawk, "Canandaigua Treaty," 43.

2. This is not intended to be an exhaustive list of all friendship belts, as such a list would be nearly impossible to assemble, given the theft of wampum belts and their housing in various museum collections. Instead, this list simply highlights some commonly known friendship belts.

3. Newman, *On Records*, 122. Newman notes that wampum "served an important function in Eastern Woodlands diplomacy, in protocols that originated among the Iroquois but were also adopted (and adapted) by Algonquian peoples."

4. Newman notes that later Euro-American scholars reversed the roles of the figures, reading the larger figure as a European with a hat instead of a Native American with a feather. Ibid., 124–25.

5. Speck, *Penn Wampum Belts*, 10–13.

6. On February 28, 2012, the Onondaga Nation filed a land claim with the federal government, and it is bringing the original Canandaigua Treaty Belt, which was commissioned by George Washington, as part of the body of evidence for their claim. Moses, "Onondaga Nation."

7. The Mohawk Nation was not physically present at this treaty, as they had largely retreated into Canada after the close of the Revolutionary War, during which they had served as allies to the British. See Venables, "Treaty."

8. Mohawk, "Canandaigua Treaty," 62. Daniel Richter describes the treaty as "deeply imbedded in the creation of a broader system of political power that, for better or worse, has shaped the lives of both Native and Euro-Americans ever since." Richter, "States," 82.

9. Articles One and Four seem to be clear reiterations of the Two Row Wampum.

10. "1795: Text of the Canandaigua Treaty," *Treaty of Canandaigua: 200 Years of Treaty Relations between the Iroquois Confederacy and the United States*: 295–98.

11. Robert Venables contends that "today's [Euro-American] generation virtually ignores this treaty. While there are many reasons why the Treaty of Canandaigua does not seem to be high on the political agenda of non-Indian governments today, one reason is national embarrassment." Venables, "Some Observations," 86.

12. Honor Indian Treaties. www.honorindiantreaties.com.

13. Indian Country Today Media Network staff, "Seneca."

14. Seneca Nation of Indians, "Seneca." Peter Jemison writes that "[a]lthough the treaty [of Canandaigua] has been violated a number of times, it has never been broken." Jemison, "Sovereignty," 154.

15. Gansworth, *Smoke Dancing*, 1. This comment is made by Fiction Tunny regarding foundational tribal stories like Sky Woman and Turtle Island; however, in the larger context of the book, her comment has a purchase from Sky Woman's moment in mythic time to contemporary community struggles at Tuscarora.

16. Teuton, "Embodying."

17. Zandy, *Hands*, xi.

18. Ibid., 1–3.

19. Rimstead, *Remnants*, 4.

20. Teuton, *Red Land*, 206–7.

21. Ibid., 208.

22. Ibid., 214.

23. Eric Gansworth observes, "Among the most frequent questions I get when doing public readings of my work is, not surprisingly, 'How did you become a writer?' It often makes me uneasy, because it seems to imply that the phrase's emphasis word could change the question's meaning significantly. For example, '*How* did you become a writer" is very different from "How did *you* become a writer" and "How did you become a *writer*" in its meaning. At least two versions of that question imply that someone in my situation—a reservation-dwelling welfare kid who grew up in a house with no plumbing and one electrical outlet—would seem an unlikely candidate to be sharing my words in public forums. . . . I suspect there are some who in fact do mean to deliver the emphasis in those dubious ways, perhaps not even aware of its tone, themselves." Gansworth, "From the Reservation," 79.

24. Sean Teuton (*Red Land*, 207) observes,

> I must work extremely hard to provide a colonial context to understand the deeper sources of poverty [in Sherman Alexie's *Reservation Blues*], which Alexie does not clearly introduce in the novel. Though we work to eliminate poverty, our experiences of it should nonetheless be accepted as a source of knowledge regarding what it means to be Native today in a community suppressed by the federal government. Crucial to this process, however, is the clarification that poverty itself is not an American Indian cultural value. Indeed, assuming as much risks leading young tribal people to internalize the dominant culture's frequent insistence that Indigenous people must remain poor in order to be spiritually pure and authentic.

25. The Tuscaroras moved from North Carolina to New York following the Tuscarora War (1711–13). They were subsequently incorporated into the Five Nations with the Oneidas as their sponsor in 1722. For more information, see Mann, *Iroquoian Women*, 41.

26. Gansworth, *Half-Life*, xvi.

27. Gansworth, e-mail correspondence with the author, December 9, 2010.

28. Gansworth, "You, Too," 25.

29. Gansworth, e-mail correspondence with the author, December 9, 2010.

30. I should note that I am referring to the unique visual code that Gansworth develops out of a variety of Hodinöhsö:ni', Native American, and popular cultural images. This visual code is distinct from the Iroquois iconography or visual code that I refer to more broadly in the present volume.

31. Gansworth, "Eric Gansworth."

32. Gansworth, *A Half-Life*, xvii. In *Iroquois Art, Power, and History*, Neal Keating (281) makes the following observation regarding Gansworth's relationship to wampum traditions: "By taking a contemporary graphic-novel approach to oral traditions, Gansworth engages the 'infinite' epistemological relations between looking at pictures and reading. This kind of engagement resonates with the Haudenosaunee performance of the reading of the wampum during the seventeenth and eighteenth centuries, when the runner both showed and spoke the information encoded in the wampum belt."

33. See also Jose Barreiro's *Thinking in Indian: A John Mohawk Reader*.

34. Dragone, unpublished manuscript.

35. Bernardin, "Seeing," 173.

36. Ibid., 177.

37. Gansworth, *Half-Life*, xvi.

38. See note 65 for more information.

39. In her essay reviewing *A Half-Life of Cardio-Pulmonary Function*, Susan Bernardin (122) refers to Gansworth's use of images from both popular and Indigenous cultures as a "cross-pollinated iconography" that "compress[es] rich, interconnected knowledge systems that bank on multiple assocations."

40. Gansworth, *Half-Life*, 1; Keating, *Iroquois Art*, 271.

41. Gansworth, *Half-Life*, xvii.

42. Wallace, *White Roots*, 51–52.

43. The passage also functions like the instruction in how to make wampum. Cornhusk dolls connect living relatives during separation much as wampum assuages grief during the separation of death.

44. Even when Bud Tunny succeeds in burning Fiction Tunny and Bertha Monterney's home to the ground along with Bertha's decades of documentary photography of her dancers, Fiction is able to reconstruct the photographic friendship chain by visiting the site of the fire with a video camera and re-narrating the dancers back into the novel's narrative thread.

45. Gansworth, *Half-Life*, 120.

46. Gansworth, *Half-Life*, 3–4.

47. In fact, this concept of surplus in a differential relationship to non-Natives is a leitmotif in Gansworth's writing. For instance, in his introductory essay for *Sovereign Bones*, Gansworth (3) compares his own experience as a poor young artist with that of amply funded non-Native artists from privileged backgrounds:

> It gradually dawned on me, after an experience in a residency program, that there are a fair number of contemporary artists who can afford to be serious about their

work because they are supported by financial institutions and cultural institutions that were long in place before they decided to pursue the work of their lives. Would they still be destroying twelve cars at once for an installation if they had to make monthly payments on those cars like everyone I know?

I still cannot fathom this liberty. I began drawing when I was three years old, on the insides of grocery bags. When I was nine or ten, my oldest brother bought me a set of watercolors for Christmas, and one of my cousins gave me a pen and ink bottle, teaching me primitive stipple techniques he had learned in a college drawing class. I got a job working as a laborer, cleaning toilets and washing vomit from school buses, when I reached the legal age to work—twelve.

When my paycheck arrived two weeks later, I bought my first-ever new pair of jeans, three canvases, three paintbrushes, a small bottle of turpentine, and as many tubes of oil paint as the cash in my pocket would allow. At the time, I lived with my mother and my uncle, in a house that had one electrical outlet box and no running water. We drank water from a hand pump outside and wired our house with strategically placed extension cords, all trailing back to that one two-plug outlet box.

48. Gansworth does not attribute a cause to the house fire, so the reader cannot reasonably assign causality to these heaters. Nonetheless, poor heating systems are a primary cause of winter house fires.

49. Gansworth, *Half-Life*, 4–5.

50. Ibid., 76.

51. Ibid., 40.

52. Ibid., 39. It is perhaps worthy of note that the Tuscarora Nation escaped implementation of the Dawes Act (1887) well into the twentieth century, as their lands were not considered to be held in trust by the United States. See Printup and Patterson, *Tuscarora Nation*, 8–9.

53. Gansworth, *Half-Life*, 99.

54. Printup and Patterson observe, "Tuscarora was enjoying what is often called the golden age of prosperity and wealth until the middle of the 20th century, when New York State disrupted the peace and brought another traumatic removal of Tuscarora people from their land." *Tuscarora Nation*, 9.

55. Gansworth, *Half-Life*, 119.

56. Ibid., 133.

57. Ibid.,16 and 132.

58. Ibid., 100–101.

59. Further, the Dish with One Spoon Belt depicts an Indigenous economy in which all eat from the same bowl; Springsteen's investment in hierarchy, which Gansworth notes in his claiming of "The Boss" as a sobriquet, makes him an allegorical figure of settler cognitive dissonance in the face of treaty agreements.

60. Gansworth, *Half-Life*, 102–3.

61. Ibid., 97.

62. Ibid., 90.

63. Neal Keating observes that Gansworth "recognizes that one cannot speak of mobilizing any Native American tradition without also locating the contexts of colonization in which it occurs." *Iroquois Art*, 280.

64. In *Smoke Dancing*, Gansworth's characters refer to "survival money" repeatedly, making it a leitmotif of economic significance: Fiction "laugh[s] at the idea of Mason Rollins hunched over some kitchen table, looping beads to get some extra survival money"; regarding employment in Smoke Rings, Big Red Harmony tells his son that "Mason Rollins is offering us survival"; about selling beadwork, Fiction notes, "A good number of folks from here do a little survival beadwork." 67, 82, and 152. This last comment also has pertinence to the economics of exchange in *Rabbit Dance*.

65. Porter, *Clanology*, 34–35. In *Clanology*, Porter describes this tripartite process:

> The Council is separated in three parts. The first part of the Council is the well and the three Rotiianéhson of the Turtle Clan sit on the north east side of the Longhouse. . . . The well is only a symbol and means that issues or problems are deposited here and remedies by the entire council are initiated or begin with the Turtle Clan leaders. These Turtle Clan leaders have the duty to arrange and prioritize the issues for presentation, review, and resolution. . . . When a resolution is formed and agreed to by the well or Turtle Clan leaders it must be sent across the council fire (Tenkatsihíia'ke) to the Wolf Clan leaders. The Wolf Clan leaders must reject or approve the pending resolution. . . . The third set of Rotiianéhson are from the Bear Clan. The Bear Clan leaders watch and listen as the issues and/ or resolutions are being heard and formulated. When the first party, Turtle Clan, second party, Wolf Clan, have all agreed, the pending resolution is then passed to the Bear Clan leaders for acceptance and ratification. Through this process, law is made.

66. Regarding individuals operating as free agents in the expression of treaty rights, Robert W. Venables writes: "in the present day, the Confederacy's debate over treaty rights with both the state of New York and the United States federal government is complicated by the fact that the national lands of each member Nation of the Confederacy are the dual responsibility of both the Confederacy and of each particular Nation. It is a complication the United States and the state of New York choose to ignore. And as individual entrepreneurs among the Haudenosaunee have created businesses and other economic endeavors on Confederacy lands, it is a complication also conveniently ignored by some of those individuals who claim to be Haudenosaunee." Venables, "Some Observations," 100. In the opinion of Ron La France, "we are looking at individuals who are taking their own rights and making them privileges. By turning these rights into privileges, they have abused their

own communities. They have abused the very, very tender threat that keeps us sovereign." La France, "Right to Sovereignty," 178.

67. Mason Rollins reflects, "Bud had a little heater on in the shed back where we could warm up, but he docked you the whole hour if you stayed more than five minutes in the shed, so most of us just bundled up and stuck it out." When Rollins confronts Bud Tunny about this issue years later, Bud still pays only two-thirds of minimum wage. Gansworth, *Smoke Dancing*, 22 and 24.

68. Anthony Wallace's division of characters in the novel into "the Business People" and the "'traditional' Chiefs' Council" gestures toward the irony that Bud Tunny is clearly a businessman himself. Wallace, *Tuscarora*, 193.

69. Gansworth, *Smoke Dancing*, 101 and 104.

70. Ibid., 110.

71. Ibid., 2.

72. Ibid., 25. When Bud Tunny tries to force Mason Rollins to close Smoke Rings, his tobacco and gasoline outfit, Mason calls into question the double standard by which only select Tuscaroras, such as the Tunnys, have the right to use their treaty rights: "You'd like me to be down on Moon Road, wouldn't you? Just drunk and passed out, shit and piss in my drawers and puke in my hair, as long as I was quiet. You could just keep running your little traditional Protestant Church government, filling your own pockets and worrying about the seventh generation of the Tunny family. Well, there are other families out here." Ibid., 30.

73. Gansworth, personal interview. Gansworth states that these were intended to be gasoline hoses.

74. Gansworth, *Smoke Dancing*, 14.

75. Horn-Miller, "Bring Us Back," 237.

76. In "Sky Woman Has Landed: Haudenosaunee Aesthetics in the Works of Eric Gansworth, Jolene Rickard, Melanie Printup Hope," Susan Bernardin discusses these kinds of aerial images and their connection to the Hodinöhsö:ni' creatrix's vision of wholeness.

77. In *Smoke Dancing* (153), Fiction makes the following comment about Sky Woman in the chapter "Fighting and Flying": "Sometimes I know why Skywoman left the Skyworld: just to have that feeling of free flight, not even worrying if something would come in time to save her or not." Significantly, the prospect of being saved, landing on Turtle's back, is clearly an economic rescue in this passage: "The rest of my life and Bert's legacy depend in part on the revenues of my first-ever yard sale."

78. Printup and Patterson, *Tuscarora Nation*, 100.

79. This was not an Indian reservation with lands held in federal trust but a "reservation" as invoked by park designer Frederick Law Olmsted.

80. Tuscarora and Friends Gallery, "200 Years of Tuscarora Beadwork."

81. In fact, Gansworth alludes to the Porter Agreement in *Smoke Dancing* (55–56): "Ruby Pem, the late Bev Harmony's mother, is one of the better-known beaders from the reservation and was an early proponent of the treaty allowing us to sell beaded souvenirs to

tourists at the parks, including Prospect Park, the biggest tourist attraction in the area—the falls itself. No one else can now do any vending at the park, unless contractually connected with the state parks department." That Fiction learns the art of Iroquois raised beadwork from Ruby Pem is also significant.

82. Gansworth's choice of Myna's name seems riddled with significance: Myna birds are "talking birds," meaning they "speak" to humans when held in captivity; they are not Indigenous to North America, but are an invasive species; they are also known for being gregarious. Like the myna bird, Myna is held in relative captivity by her boyfriend Eddie, and she mindlessly parrots back his words and those of others without interrogating their actual meaning. Rhoda and Flossie stage an intellectual intervention, insofar as they teach Myna how to respond more critically to the narrative of her existence as a young, white female, and help her in dismantling the inculcation she received from her boyfriend, father, teachers, and other influential figures.

83. Gansworth, *Rabbit Dance*, 2.

84. Ibid., 10–11.

85. Ibid., 8.

86. Ibid., 6. Myna further illustrates her market savvy when she considers the beaded jitterbugs and assesses their value: "I can see why these would move." Ibid., 11.

87. Ibid., 9–10.

88. Ibid., 8.

89. Flossie says, "They found her snagged in the rocks, not too far from here. Still in the upper rapids. . . . Like the Maid of the Mist, another sacrifice." Ibid., 30.

90. Ibid., 36.

91. Albers, "From Legend," 269.

3. Tribal Feminist Recuperation of the Mother of Nations in Shelley Niro's *Kissed by Lightning*: A Rematriating Reading of the Women's Nomination Belt

1. Beverley Jacobs appears in Dawn Martin-Hill's documentary film *Sewatokwa'tshera't*.

2. Sources vary on the actual date of the Peacemaker's journey and the formation of the Confederacy. Barbara Mann and Jerry Fields estimate that the Confederacy was formed circa AD 1142, based on astronomical evidence. Other scholars place the formation of the league between this date and 1600. "A Sign in the Sky," 105.

3. Gibson, *Concerning the League*, xix. My recounting of the Peacemaker epic relies primarily upon this version of Gibson's rendition of the Great Law of Peace, which is considered to be more definitive than the version translated by Goldenweiser or Hewitt. Meanwhile, the Chiefs' official version of the Great Law is influenced by Gibson's presence, as well. Peter Jemison (Seneca), who is chief administrator of the Ganondagan Historic Site, located at the Mother of Nations' home village, prefers the Gibson version of the Great Law to others for its accuracy in portraying the Mother of Nations.

4. Wallace, *White Roots of Peace*, 22. Hanni Woodbury translates this name to mean "Fat Face." Gibson, *Concerning the League*, xxi.

5. The Centre for Arab Genomic Studies' *Catalogue for Transmission Genetics in Arabs Database* notes that "Supernumerary teeth, or hyperdontia are the existing of additional teeth to the normal series in the dental arches. It occurs with both primary and permanent teeth, but it is more common with permanent teeth. . . . Many supernumerary teeth never erupt and these may delay eruption of nearby teeth *or cause other dental problems* [emphasis mine]. . . . In the Caucasian population, the incidence of supernumerary teeth ranges from 1–3%, and the highest frequency has been in found in Native American tribes." To date, it appears that a wide-ranging study of Native American incidence of supernumerary dentition has not been conducted; however, based on colloquial information gathered amongst Native Americans whom I know and their families, supernumerary dentition occurs quite frequently. Thus, the attribution of the Peacemaker's speech impediment to an entire double row of permanent incisors seems plausible, though cleft lips occur in Native communities with relative frequency as well. Nonetheless, the Peacemaker's name does not connect to a cleft lip or palate in translation. Barbara Alice Mann notes that the Peacemaker's speech impediment might also have been a stutter or an accent caused by speaking "a northern dialect," resulting from his origins in the Wendat Territory on the north end of Lake Ontario. *Iroquoian Women*, 38.

6. Barbara Alice Mann writes that "[t]he Clan Mothers of the villages had an ancient obligation to sit at the crossroads of war and feed passing war parties of any and all sides in return for their villages being left unharmed." *Iroquoian Women*, 37.

7. Wallace, *White Roots of Peace*, 41.

8. Needless to say, there are numerous versions of the Peacemaker story; however, I have tried to stick to the most common versions. The story itself contains a great deal more subtlety, nuance, and significance for Hodinöhsö:ni' political structure; however, my interest here is to recount the Mother of Nations' history and to contextualize her acts within the larger structure of the Peacemaker epic.

9. Peter Jemison notes that "[s]ome versions [of the Great Law] do not mention her at all." He also identifies Ganondagan as the site of the Mother of Nations' village. Jemison, "Mother of Nations," 69 and 68.

10. In the preface to Arthur C. Parker's *The Life of General Ely S. Parker*, "F.H.S." refers to the Mother of Nations as the "Peace Queen" and attributes her tribal identity to the Neutrals. ix.

11. Mann, *Iroquoian Women*, 36–38.

12. Porter (Sakokweniónkwas), *And Grandma Said*, 290–91. Porter states, "She [the Mother of Nations] was a manipulative woman. A very controlling woman. She knew medicine, and she had the power to do things. Even to take people's life through medicine, if she wanted to. She had medicine that was like love medicine too. If she saw a man and wanted that man, she could fix medicine on him and she'd get him." Ibid., 290.

13. In his revised version of Seth Newhouse's *Constitution of the Confederacy by the Peace-maker*, Chief Jacob E. Thomas omits any mention of the Mother of Nations.

14. Doxtator, "Godi'Nigoha'," 29. Tom Hill observes, "Our discussion [of Godi'Nigoha' in organizing the Woodland Cultural Centre exhibit] centered on a repeated phrase from the Ganohonyohk (the Thanksgiving Address); the phrase *netogye:' niyohoto:k ogwa'nigoha* translated as *Be it so, it remains in your minds*. Besides being an admonition, the phrase also conceptualized the notion that the natural world is integral to our intellectual process. The mind and the land are one." Hill continues by identifying the Western intellectual tradition as a source of "devaluing whatever is associated with women and nature" and calling for an investigation of "these relationships from a woman's perspective and return to our Iroquoian traditions and philosophy." Hill, *Godi'Nigoha'*, 6.

15. Martin, "Shelley Niro," 61. Allan Ryan writes, "What distinguishes much of Niro's photography in particular is a sense of humor brought into sharp (and sometimes soft) focus in witty self-portraits and comical studies of family members. She captures a playful energy missing from so many archival images." Ryan, "I Enjoy," 44.

16. Martin, "Shelley Niro," 61.

17. Heckewelder describes women's roles in dissuading men from going to war and in maintaining peace. Heckewelder, *History, Manner, and Customs*, 57–58.

18. Arthur Parker designates Oniagara as the original village of one of the earlier Mother of Nations, the name being inherited with each generation; however, when the Haudenosaunee warred with and absorbed the Cultivators, "the Mother of Nations was made a Seneca." Thus, the Mother of Nations' home village became Ganondagan. Parker, *Life of General Ely S. Parker*, 45–46.

19. Gray, "Ka'shastensera."

20. Mavis's surname Dogblood alludes to the White Dog Ceremony, which is no longer practiced.

21. Mann, *Iroquoian Women*, 37.

22. Parker notes that there are strong associations between the Mother of Nations and wampum; in fact, she was regularly gifted Peace Belts by warriors traveling along the path that went by her village. Parker, *Life of General Ely S. Parker*, 45.

23. Barbara Alice Mann (*Iroquoian Women*, 116–17) states:

> The *gantowisas* enjoyed sweeping political powers, which ranged from the administrative and legislative to the judicial. The *gantowisas* ran the local clan councils. They held all the lineage wampum, nomination belts, and titles. They ran the funerals. They retained exclusive rights over naming, i.e., the creation of new citizens and the installation of public officials. They nominated all male sachems as well as Clan Mothers to office and retained the power to impeach wrongdoers. They appointed warriors, declared war, negotiated peace, and mediated disputes.
>
> Notwithstanding these stunning facts, academic discussions of the League as a political entity almost exclusively concentrate on the men's Grand Council.

The contrapuntal Clan Mothers' councils are studiously ignored, not because they were unimportant to the League (or to other Iroquoian governments) but because western scholars are following the prescriptions of male dominance so central to Europeans political history.

24. Additionally, placing Mavis and Kateri in opposition to each other instead of a female/male struggle obviates the reduction of the plotline to a gender struggle as well as stereotypes of aboriginal men as abusive.

25. Keating, *Iroquois Art*, 269.

26. Neal Keating has observed that in Niro's work "decolonization requires healing." Ibid., 268. Similarly, in *Kissed by Lightning*, Mavis must grieve and heal, in order to reclaim the powers incumbent upon her as a literal and metaphoric clanmother.

27. I have previously discussed this sequence in *It Starts with a Whisper* at length. See Kelsey, "Condolence and Iroquois Visual Narrative."

28. Raheja, *Reservation Reelism*, 179.

29. In fact, the prominence of the paintings throughout the film is noteworthy, and perhaps can be explained by Niro's own observation that "she finds painting to be more liberating than photography or beadwork." Keating, *Iroquois Art*, 269.

30. See Medak-Saltzman, unpublished manuscript.

31. In *Reservation Reelism*, Raheja makes the following observation: "*It Starts with a Whisper* also engages in what might more usefully be called 'prophetic hope' by hinging not on an individual leader but by demonstrating the work of prophecy from the ground up. Rather than relying on a messianic figure or divine intervention, as do millennial and eschatological belief systems, the film reads the Indigenous body itself as a prophetic text. The film prophesizes an omnitemporal new beginning that takes place simultaneously in several different time/space continuums" (180). This same "prophetic hope," as here defined by Raheja, seems to be operative in other work by Shelley Niro, including *Kissed by Lightning*.

32. Penn-Hilden, *Writing from a Red Zone*, 11–12.

33. Fenton and Wright, "Seneca Indians," 313.

4. Kahnawake's Reclamation of Adoption Practices in Tracey Deer's Documentary and Fiction Films: Reading the Adoption Belt in a Post-Indian Act Era

1. Hubert Skye (Faithkeeper, Cayuga Nation, Snipe Clan) appears in Martin-Hill, *Sewatokwa'tshera't*.

2. Sarah Hamill writes, "Prior to Bill C-31, Indian status could be gained or lost in a number of ways which disproportionately affected women. . . . Prior to 1985, a woman with Indian status would lose status and band membership if she married a non-status man; a woman without Indian status [i.e., legally white] would gain it if she married a status man. Those women who lost status would not regain it upon divorce, and those women who gained status would keep it if they got divorced. The only way a woman could change her status was if she remarried. Male status was unaffected by marriage." "*McIvor v Canada*," 75.

The Native Women's Association of Canada's "Guide to Bill C-31" (3–4) makes the inherent gender bias of this legislation clear:

All status Indians are now categorized as falling under section 6(1) or 6(2) of the *Indian Act*. The major distinction between 6(1) and 6(2) status is that people classified in the latter category cannot transmit their status to their children. The following scenario depicts a very simple but clear example of the impact of the new classifications. A woman who lost her status upon marriage to a non-Indian man can apply for reinstatement and regain her status under section 6(1): her children are then classified as having 6(2) status, but her grandchildren are not entitled to status. Second generation descendants must have both parents registered under section 6(1) or (2), or at least one parent with 6(1) status, in order to be registered. This also applies to the registration of future generations, thereby establishing a cut-off point for determining status, as well as creating two distinct classes of Indian status—one which allows for the direct transmission of status to children, and one which does not. Through Bill C-31, the *Indian Act* was amended to ensure that no one gains or loses status through marriage, and individuals who lost status through sexual discrimination and enfranchisement can apply to regain their status. . . . While the overtly discriminatory provisions have been removed from the *Indian Act* through Bill C-31, the new system of distinguishing between and classifying types of Indian status means that discrimination has been maintained.

In many ways the reinscription of patriarchy into Bill C-31 continues the cultural genocidal policy of the Indian Act, as it runs entirely counter to traditional Hodinöhsö:ni' reckoning of identity via matrilineal descent. Bill C-31 poses a second disruption to this Indigenous practice of identity formation.

3. Sharon Donna McIvor writes, "Since 1869, colonialist and patriarchal federal laws—most notably the *Indian Act*—have fostered patriarchy in Aboriginal communities and subjected Aboriginal women to loss of Indian status and the benefits of band membership, eviction from reserve homes, and denial of an equal share of matrimonial property. Colonialism and patriarchy have also enabled cooperation between male Aboriginal leadership and Canadian governments to resist the inclusion of Aboriginal women in Aboriginal governance. These denials and exclusions perpetuate the exposure of Aboriginal women and their children to violence and consign many to poverty." "Aboriginal Women Unmasked," 106–7.

4. Shari Huhndorf and Cheryl Suzack observe that "Status Indian women in Canada are up to five times more likely than other women to die of violence, and their counterparts in the United States are 2.5 times more likely than non-Indigenous women to be raped." "Indigenous Feminism," 5. Similar patterns of violence against Indigenous women extend south into Latin America as well. See Smith, *Conquest*.

5. At the time of this book going to press, Deer and Bonspiel have separated and have filed for divorce. The former couple has negotiated for *The Eastern Door* to go to Bonspiel as part of the settlement, as he is a journalist primarily by trade.

6. Huhndorf, *Mapping the Americas*, 11–12.

7. Sunseri, *Being Again of One Mind*, 2–3. Sunseri identifies "decolonizing nationalist movements [as] those aimed at forming new relationships that break away from colonialist structures of governance and that are rooted in notions of nationhood and sovereignty" which are "inclusive and based . . . on a consensus-based decision-making model and, quite important, on gender balance." Ibid., 3. Deer's film manages to perform exactly this kind of separation from colonialist structures and rearticulation of a communitarian and gender-egalitarian model of determining identity that is rooted in the Great Law (i.e., clanmothers' powers).

8. Askeland, "Informal Adoption," 5–6.

9. Mary Jemison describes this period of character evaluation in detail in *Narrative of the Life of Mrs. Mary Jemison*. This discussion of adoption practices focuses on sources originating within Hodinöhsö:ni' culture, whether affiliated by birth or adoption, as many of the non-Native histories written about these practices ground themselves in assumptions that forward a trajectory of empire and settlement, thereby calling into question their accuracy.

10. Tom Porter notes, "In Akwesasne, some people regard the Rotihshennakéhte as a clan, but in fact they are not a clan. They are a certain identifiable group of people who do not have a clan. They become the carriers of the name of whichever clan adopts them. Many years ago, when our people were attacked and killed, our ancestors would go to the place where they lost people and capture women, men, and children to replace the lost ones. These captives, non-Native and Native, were adopted and married into the Mohawks. They and their offspring were, and still are, called the people of Rotihshennakéhte ['They carry the name']." *And Grandma Said*, 107.

11. Muller, "Two 'Mystery' Belts," 134.

12. Parker, *Life of General Ely S. Parker*, 329–31. Citing Barbara Alice Mann, Lori Askeland argues that these adoptions of outsiders were sometimes "a diplomatic gesture . . . [without] adoption into a specific family, clan, or the Confederacy as a whole." She continues, "In virtually all cases, the needs of the community for continuity and lineage were of primary importance." "Informal Adoption," 6.

13. Snow, Gehring, and Starna, *In Mohawk Country*, 47 and 62. This list is intended to be illustrative, rather than exhaustive.

14. Parker, *Life of General Ely S. Parker*, 331. Regarding the actual adoption ceremony, Parker provides the following description:

> Three persons are always adopted at a time. Sometimes, in compliment, an Indian name is bestowed; but this is not adoption. The ceremony is explained to the writer by a Seneca friend as follows:

An Indian friend allows his name to be given to the white. This admits to his clan. This part is executed by the mothers of the clan. The assemblage is informed of the agreement, whereupon two aged Indians take the candidate by the hand and walk with him, followed by his clan. The other clans rise and bow in reverence to the Creator, with the left hand uplifted, the right hand over the heart. The mothers clap hands in cadence with the chant sung by the old men as they lead the candidate around the council-fire, the assemblage responding, *Hae, hae*." This brings out the wholly serious and reverential character of the ancient ceremony. As now performed, the details vary according to circumstances, but always certain essentials are observed. There is always an address given, on the Cattaraugus reservation, in Seneca, stating the reasons for adoption in the particular case, the clans and persons adopting, and the name to be given; second, the welcome in which the candidate is escorted up and down the council-house, or before the assemblage, by two chiefs, the chiefs chanting and the people responding. A general greeting and exchange of gifts follow.

15. Speaker's Corner interviewees include Roberta Kelly, Peter Taylor, Andrea Meloche, John Dee Delormier, Timmy Norton, Alexandra Cross, Tammy Beauvais, Deidre Diome, Carol Jacas, Alex M. McComber, Keith Myiow, Brenda Dearhouse Fragnito, Tiorahkwathe Gilbert, Patricia Bush Stacey, Julia Montour, Kevin John Saylor, Elizabeth Curotte, Cecilia Charlie, Nancy Diabo, Rita McComber, Rebecca Scott, Kaneratiio, Kahehtiio Diabo, and Gregory Angus.

16. As Alex McComber notes in *Club Native*, the Indian Act and the tribal rolls associated with it were intended to do away with tribal identity through enfranchisement: "The Indian Act is one of the most oppressive pieces of legislation that exists in any country in the world as far as I'm concerned. South Africa used it as a model to set up their apartheid system . . . It's a racist, assimilationist piece of legislation all wrapped up in this nice big bow that says we're gonna do things for you."

Joyce Green ("Don't Tell Us," 166) expands upon this analysis: "Recognition by the state, or 'status,' always has been a tool of the colonial government intended to identify a discrete community for policy attention—the ultimate objective of which was assimilation—and to limit the financial liability of the state." Similarly, in the United States, some tribal individuals specifically resisted being added to the "base rolls" because they anticipated that being enumerated would be a tool for enacting cultural genocide. In *Real Indians*, Eva Marie Garroutte (22) observes, "The effort, in a nutshell, was to destroy indigenous cultures by destroying their foundation—their collective ownership of land—and then to integrate the Indians thus 'liberated' into the dominant American culture. Through a process of land allotment, Indians were to be remade into individual, private owners of small farms who would quickly become independent of government attention and expenditures."

17. I mark changes in speaker through contrastive use of italics and roman type.

18. The omission of mentioning matrilineal descent may be reflective of the internalization of patriarchal norms via the Indian Act or may be due to the extensive intermixing of Kahnawake Mohawks with the surrounding non-Native community, which has resulted in a complex of factors being accounted for in designating an individual *Kanien'kehá:ka* or non-Native.

19. Mitchell, "Mohawks in High Steel," 10–11.

20. For further explanation of the term "Iahti-Ongwehonwe," see Dickson-Gilmore, "Iati-Ongwehonwe," 27–43. Dickson-Gilmore historicizes and outlines at length the processes by which Mohawk citizenship and membership (i.e., being Ögwe'öweh) has been determined in the past and present. In brief, blood quantum, lineal descent, and cultural identity have all played more or less important roles at different times; however, even presently, there is no uniform consensus as to what constitutes an Ögwe'öweh individual. Concomitantly, there is not uniform consensus about what constitutes a Iati-Onkwehonwe or non-Onkwehonwe individual.

21. Simpson, "On Ethnographic Refusal," 77–78.

22. Ibid., 76.

23. Deer's documentary work is further extended by her independent and mainstream fictional films, *Escape Hatch* and *Mohawk Girls: On Reserve*. Through fictional techniques Deer is able to creatively portray the emotional impact of Kahnawake Mohawk women's struggles to find a suitable Native partner. Deer describes *Escape Hatch* in a written pitch as follows: "[It] centres around Bailey (the busy Kaniehtioo Horn), Caitlin (Heather White), Zoe (Brittany Leborgne) and Anna (Maika Harper), four twenty-something Mohawk women trying to find their place in the world, and of course, trying to find love. But in a small world where you or your friends have dated everyone on the 'rez,' or the hot new guy turns out to be your cousin, it ain't that simple. Torn between family pressure, tradition, obligation and the intoxicating freedom of the 'outside world,' this fabulous foursome is on a mission to find happiness . . . and find themselves."

The silent scream of Kaniehtiio Horn's character at the close of *Escape Hatch* succinctly embodies that Catch-22 of only being allowed to date, partner, and reproduce with an acceptable, Native man who is either a first or second cousin or is already partnered.

24. Eva Marie Garroutte (*Real Indians*, 21) recounts a similar event at the Onondaga Nation: "In 1974, the tribal council ordered all noncitizens to leave the reservation or face ejection. This order even included noncitizen spouses (who were mostly women) and the children born to Onondaga men by such women. The Onondaga men could stay, of course—but only if they chose to live apart from their wives and mixed-race children."

25. One of the interviewees is a woman who lost status because of marrying a non-Native man: "I love being a Mohawk person. I love Kahnawake. When I go home to Chateaugay and I cross that bridge, I always feel bad. I *feel bad in my heart* that I can't be here. This is my home too. I never considered Chateaugay my home." Another woman attempted to move home and was subjected to vandalism and harassment; she states that she could

not face the emotional duress and moved away as a result. In a voiceover, Deer asserts that women bear the brunt of this treatment: "for men who married out, it was a different story" and "One big issue [with the Kahnawake Membership Law (2004) was gender inequality." A man, Alex McComber, who remembers the late-night raids of the 1970s, makes the following statement about the current political climate: "People were going around and, you know, standing in front of somebody's house saying 'get out. You don't belong here,' and this and that. There was someone in my neighborhood who was in that situation who could have been visited, and I always thought to myself that if that gang of people showed up at their house, I'd go out there with my hose and squirt them down and chase them away." Clearly, the community opinion is not of one mind on this topic.

26. Audra Simpson observes, "'Mohawk' and 'nationhood' are inseparable. Both are simply about *being*. Being is about who you are, and a sense of who you are is arrived at through your relationship with other people—your people." Quoted in Alfred, *Peace, Power, Righteousness*, 5.

27. Scott Lyons, *X-Marks*, 35–36.

28. Silko, "Yellow Woman."

29. Valaskakis, *Indian Country*, 218.

30. Garroutte, 12.

31. Ibid., 14.

32. Ibid., 39.

33. Ibid., 42. Even scholars as far-flung as Elizabeth Cook-Lynn agree with Garroutte on this point. In "Literary and Political Questions of Transformation: American Indian Fiction Writers," Cook-Lynn (49) states, "To adopt this idea [of racial purity] in its fullest, most sophisticated sense makes hybridity a contaminant to the American Indian's right to authenticity."

34. Garroutte, 100.

35. In fact, a working group specific to the Membership Law has been formed to address how to best revise the process as part of the Kahnawà:ke Community Decisionmaking Process. Jean Dennison has studied the issue of enrollment and headrights in a groundbreaking study, *Colonial Entanglement: Constituting a Twenty-First-Century Osage Nation*. Dennison describes her project as laying bare "how constitutional writing is a process that attempts to fuse various histories, meanings, identities, and bodies, creating new material and political realities. . . . I aim to expose the possibilities, limitations, and consequences of such a coalescing process, as articulated by variously situated Osage" (5).

36. Garroutte, 101.

37. I would note that Deer has been instrumental in speaking out in community meetings on the membership issue at Kahnawake and has consistently sought conciliatory methods for resolving the community dispute over these concerns. Additionally, Deer has written for, edited, and published *The Eastern Door*, a Kahnawake community newspaper, and the paper, under her leadership and that of her husband Steve Bonspiel, has sought

to propagate perspective that facilitate dialogue regarding "hot button" issues and strive for inclusiveness in defining membership. Finally, Deer has also founded and led a Kahnawake women's group that has focused on issues specific to women from the community, including issues surrounding selection of partners and its impact on women's quality of life and ability to participate in the community.

38. Griffin, "Tracey Deer."

39. Taiaiake, *Wasáse*, 34.

5. Conclusion: Wampum and the Future of Hodinöhsö:ni' Narrative Epistemology

1. This claim is not intended to dismiss the significance of continuous wampum traditions that are carried from generation to generation by a trained cadre of wampum keepers. As Richard W. Hill Sr. reports, even in cases where wampum belts have been stolen and separated from communities for generations, he has found that the knowledge held in the belts is recoverable. See Hill, "Regenerating Identity."

2. In fact, while Deer's documentary is specifically grounded in the context of Kahnawake, a number of concerns around women, reproduction, status, and the right to live on-territory are commonly held in Hodinöhsö:ni' nations that treat with Canada. Further, similar concerns, especially with regard to enrollment, partnership, and reproduction, also impact Ögwe'öweh women in nations that treat with the United States, though the specific variations in how these contested zones of identity formation play out vary considerably from community to community (i.e., Tonawanda Band of Senecas versus Seneca-Cayuga Nation).

3. Fadden originally began publishing in the 1950s under the pen name Aren Akweks.

4. Toensing, "Mohawk Man Accused."

Bibliography

Albers, Patricia C. "From Legend to Land to Labor: Changing Perspectives on Native American Work." In *Native Americans and Wage Labor: Ethnohistorical Perspectives*, edited by Alice Littlefield and Martha C. Knack, 245–73. Norman: University of Oklahoma Press, 1996.

Alfred, Taiaiake. *Peace, Power, Righteousness: An Indigenous Manifesto*. Don Mills, ON: Oxford University Press, 2009.

———. *Wasáse: Indigenous Pathways of Action and Freedom*. Toronto, ON: University of Toronto Press, 2009.

Askeland, Lori. "Informal Adoption, Apprentices, and Indentured Children in the Colonial Era and the New Republic, 1605–1850." In *Children and Youth in Adoption, Orphanages, and Foster Care: A Historical Handbook and Guide*, edited by Lori Askeland, 3–16. Westport, CT: Greenwood, 2006.

Baehr, H. W. *The New York Tribune since the Civil War*. New York: Octagon Books, 1972.

Bardeau, Phyllis Eileen Williams. *Definitive Seneca: It's in the Word*. Edited by Jaré Cardinal. Salamanca, NY: Seneca-Iroquois National Museum, 2011.

Barreiro, Jose. *Thinking in Indian: A John Mohawk Reader*. Golden, CO: Fulcrum, 2011.

Bernardin, Susan. "As Long as the Hair Shall Grow: Survivance in Eric Gansworth's Reservation Fictions." In *Survivance: Narratives of Native Presence*, edited by Gerald Vizenor, 123–45. Lincoln: University of Nebraska Press, 2008.

———. Review of *A Half Life of Cardio-Pulmonary Function: Poems and Paintings*, by Eric Gansworth. *Studies in American Indian Literatures* 22, no. 1 (Spring 2010): 121–25.

———. "Seeing Memory, Storying Memory: Printup Hope, Rickard, Gansworth." In *Native American Visualities*, edited by Denise Cummings, 161–88. East Lansing: Michigan State University Press, 2011.

———. "Sky Woman Has Landed: Haudenosaunee Aesthetics in the Works of Eric Gansworth, Jolene Rickard, Melanie Printup Hope." Paper presented at the Native American Literature Symposium, Soaring Eagle Casino and Resort, Mt. Pleasant, Michigan, March 10, 2007.

Canfield, William W. *The Legends of the Iroquois Told by "The Cornplanter."* Port Washington, NY: Ira J. Friedman, 1971.

Centre for Arab Genomic Studies: A Division of Sheikh Hamdan Award for Medical Sciences. "Teeth, Supernumerary." In *Catalogue for Transmission Genetics in Arabs Database.* http://www.cags.org.ae/ctga_search.html.

Colden, Cadwallader. *The History of the Five Nations.* Ithaca, NY: Cornell University Press, 1958.

Cook-Lynn, Elizabeth. "Literary and Political Questions of Transformation: American Indian Fiction Writers." *Wicazo Sa Review* 11, no. 1 (Spring 1995): 49.

Deer, Tracey. *Club Native* (film). 2008.

————. *Escape Hatch* (film). 2009.

————. *Kanien'kehàka/Living the Language* (film). 2008.

————. *Mohawk Girls* (film). 2005.

————. *Mohawk Girls* (pilot episode of series for the Aboriginal Peoples Television Network [APTN]). 2009.

Deer, Tracey, with Cynthia Knight. *Crossing the Line* (film). 2009.

Dennison, Jean. *Colonial Entanglement: Constituting a Twenty-First-Century Osage Nation.* Chapel Hill: University of North Carolina Press, 2012.

Diamond, Neil, with Tracey Deer. *One More River: The Deal that Split the Cree* (film). Outremount, QC: Rezolution Pictures, 2005.

Dickson-Gilmore, D. J. "Iati-Ongwehonwe: Blood Quantum, Membership and the Politics of Exclusion in Kahnawake." *Citizenship Studies* 3, no. 1 (1999): 27–43.

Dowling, Sarah. "'And Through Its Naming Became Owner': Translation in James Thomas Stevens' *Tokinish.*" *GLQ: A Journal of Lesbian and Gay Studies* 16, nos. 1–2 (2010): 191–206.

Doxtator, Deborah. "Godi'Nigoha': The Women's Mind and Seeing through to the Land." In *Godi'Nigoha': The Women's Mind,* by Deborah Doxtator, 29–43. Brantford, ON: Woodland Cultural Centre, 1997.

Dragone, Nicholle. "The Good Mind" (working title). Unpublished essay written as part of comprehensive exams for the Ph.D. program in American Studies at the State University of New York, Buffalo. N.d.

Driskill, Qwo-Li, Chris Finley, Brian Joseph Gilley, and Scott Lauria Morgensen, eds. "Introduction." In *Queer Indigenous Studies: Critical Interventions in Theory, Politics, and Literature.* Tucson: University of Arizona Press, 2011.

Fadden, Ray Tehanetorens. *Legends of the Iroquois*. Summertown, TN: The Book Publishing Company, 1998.

Fenton, William N. "Return of Eleven Wampum Belts to the Six Nations Iroquois Confederacy on Grand River, Canada." *Ethnohistory* 36, no. 4 (1989): 392–410.

———, and Asher Wright. "Seneca Indians by Asher Wright (1859)." *Ethnohistory* 4, no. 3 (1957): 302–21.

Gansworth, Eric. *A Half-Life of Cardiopulmonary Function*. Syracuse, NY: Syracuse University Press, 2008.

———. E-mail correspondence. December 9, 2010.

———. "Eric Gansworth: Writer & Visual Artist." http://www.ericgansworth .com. Accessed December 3, 2010.

———. "From the Reservation to *Dawn of the Dead* to James Dickey and Back Again." In *Sovereign Bones: New Native American Writing*, edited by Eric Gansworth, 79–88. New York: Nation Books, 2007.

———. "Introduction." In *Sovereign Bones: New Native American Writing*, edited by Eric Gansworth, 1–9. New York: Nation Books, 2007.

———. Personal interview with the author, September 24, 2010.

———. *Rabbit Dance* (play). Unpublished manuscript. N.d.

———. *Smoke Dancing*. East Lansing: Michigan State University Press, 2004.

———. "You, Too, Will Have This Printed Word (World) of Your Own." In *Strawberries in Brooklyn: Maurice Kenny Considered*, edited by Penelope Kelsey, 15–25. Albany: State University of New York Press, 2011.

Garroutte, Eva Marie. *Real Indians: Identity and the Survival of Native America*. Berkeley: University of California Press, 2003.

Gibson, John Arthur. *Concerning the League: The Iroquois League Tradition as Dictated in Onondaga*. Translated by Hanni Woodbury. Syracuse, NY: Syracuse University Press, 1992.

Gilbert, Alan. "A Review of *A Bridge Dead in the Water* by James Thomas Stevens; Central Question: Is the Disease Part of the Cure?" *The Believer*, May 2007. London: Salt Publishing, 2007. http://www.believermag.com/issues /200705/?read=review_stevens.

Goeman, Mishuana. "Notes toward a Native Feminism's Spatial Practice." *Wicazo Sa Review* 24, no. 2 (2009): 169–87.

Gray, Kanatiiosh Barbara Ann. "Ka'shastensera Kontiha:we'ne Iotiianeh:shon: The Women's Nomination Belt: Explanation of Symbols." Peace 4 Turtle Island website. http://www.peace4turtleisland.org/pages/womensbelt.htm. Accessed February 7, 2011.

Green, Joyce. "Don't Tell Us Who We Are (Not): Reflections on Métis Identity." *Aboriginal Policy Studies* 1, no. 2 (2011): 166–70.

Griffin, John. "Not Just a Filmmaker—A Publisher, Too." *Montreal Gazette*, December 5, 2009. Accessed May 18, 2011.

———. "Tracey Deer Is Shattering Stereotypes." *Montreal Gazette*, December 5, 2009. Accessed May 18, 2011.

Haas, Angela. "Wampum as Hypertext: An American Indian Intellectual Tradition of Multimedia Theory and Practice." *Studies in American Indian Literatures* 19, no. 4 (2007): 77–100.

Hamill, Sarah E. "*McIvor v. Canada* and the 2010 Amendments to the *Indian Act*: A Half-Hearted Remedy to Historical Injustice." *Constitutional Forum Constitutionnel* 19, no. 2 (2011): 75–84.

Heckewelder, John. *History, Manner, and Customs of the Indian Nations Who Once Inhabited Pennsylvania and the Neighboring States*. Westminster, MD: Heritage, 2007.

Higginson, Catherine. "Shelley Niro, Haudenosaunee Nationalism, and the Continued Contestation of the Brant Monument." *Essays on Canadian Writing* 80 (2003): 141–88.

Hill, Greg. "Fluid Identities: Learning to Swim." In *IroquoisART: Visual Expressions of Contemporary Native American Artists*, edited by Sylvia S. Kasprycki, Doris I. Stambrau, and Alexandra V. Roth, 40–47. Frankfurt, Germany: Amerika Haus, 1998.

Hill, Richard W., Sr. "Regenerating Identity: Repatriation and the Indian Frame of Mind." In *The Future of the Past: Archaeologists, Native Americans, and Repatriation*, edited by Tamara L. Bray, 127–38. New York: Routledge, 2001.

Hill, Tom. "Preface and Acknowledgements." In *Godi'Nigoha': The Women's Mind*, by Deborah Doxtator, 6–7. Brantford, ON: Woodland Cultural Centre, 1997.

Hladki, Janice. "Decolonizing Colonial Violence: The Subversive Practices of Aboriginal Film and Video." *Canadian Woman Studies* 25, nos. 1–2 (2006): 83–87.

Honor Indian Treaties. www.honorindiantreaties.com. Accessed November 30, 2010.

hooks, bell. *Talking Back: Thinking Feminist, Thinking Black*. Boston: South End, 1989.

Horn-Miller, Kahente, "Bring Us Back into the Dance: Women of the Wasase." In *Colonize This! Young Women of Color on Today's Feminism*, edited by Daisy Hernández and Bushra Rehman, 230–44. New York: Seal Press, 2002.

Huhndorf, Shari. *Mapping the Americas*. Ithaca, NY: Cornell University Press, 2009.

Huhndorf, Shari M., and Cheryl Suzack. "Indigenous Feminism: Theorizing the Issues." In *Indigenous Women and Feminism: Politics, Activism, Culture*, edited by Cheryl Suzack, Shari M. Huhndorf, Jeanne Perreault, and Jean Barman, 1–17. Vancouver: University of British Columbia Press, 2011.

Indian Country Today Media Network staff. "Seneca Indian Nation Pursues Hydropower License." *Indian Country Today*, December 15, 2010.

Jemison, G. Peter. "Mother of Nations—The Peace Queen: A Neglected Tradition." *Akwe:kon* (1988): 68–70.

———. "Sovereignty & Treaty Rights—We Remember." In *Treaty of Canandaigua 1794: 200 Years of Treaty Relations between the Iroquois Confederacy and the United States*, edited by G. Peter Jemison and Anna M. Schein, 148–61. Santa Fe, NM: Clear Light, 2000.

Jemison, G. Peter, and Anna M. Schein, eds. *Treaty of Canandaigua 1794: 200 Years of Treaty Relations between the Iroquois Confederacy and the United States*. Santa Fe, NM: Clear Light, 2000.

Johansen, Bruce Elliot, ed. *Enduring Legacies: Native American Treaties and Contemporary Controversies*. Santa Barbara, CA: Praeger, 2004.

Johnson, Jay T., Renee Pualani Louis, and Albertus Promano. "Facing the Future: Encouraging Critical Cartographic Literacies in Indigenous Communities." *ACME: An International E-Journal for Critical Cartographies* 4, no. 1 (2006): 80–98.

Kalant, Amelia. *National Identity and the Conflict at Oka: Native Belonging and Myths of Postcolonial Nationhood in Canada*. New York: Routledge, 2004.

Kalter, Susan, ed. *Benjamin Franklin, Pennsylvania, and the First Nations: The Treaties of 1736–62*. Champaign-Urbana: University of Illinois Press, 2006.

Keating, Neal. *Iroquois Art, Power, and History*. Norman: University of Oklahoma Press, 2012.

Kelsey, Penelope Myrtle. "Condolence and Iroquois Visual Narrative: Tribal Theory in Shelley Niro and Anna Gronau's *It Starts with a Whisper*." In *Visualities: Perspectives on Contemporary American Indian Art and Film*, edited by Denise K. Cummings, 119–30. Lansing: Michigan State University Press, 2011.

———. "Gathering the Threads Together: Urban/Diasporic/Multitribal Native North American Narratives in Nationalist Theory." In *Comparative Indigeneities of the Américas: Toward a Hemispheric Approach*, edited by M. Bianet Castellanos, Lourdes Gutiérrez Nájera, and Arturo J. Aldama, 23–37. Tucson: University of Arizona Press, 2012.

Krehbiehl, Henry Edward. "The Iroquois Wampum: An Ancient Treasure that Has Disappeared." *New-York Tribune Illustrated Supplement*, July 8, 1897, 9.

http://chroniclingamerica.loc.gov/lccn/sn83030214/1897-07-11/ed-1/seq-31
.pdf.

La France, Ron. "The Right to Sovereignty." In *Treaty of Canandaigua 1794: 200 Years of Treaty Relations between the Iroquois Confederacy and the United States*, edited by G. Peter Jemison and Anna M. Schein, 175–82. Santa Fe, NM: Clear Light, 2000.

Lyons, Oren. "Indian Self-Government in the Haudenosaunee Constitution." *Nordic Journal International* 55 (1986): 119.

———. "The Canandaigua Treaty: A View from the Six Nations." In *Treaty of Canandaigua, 1794: 200 Years of Treaty Relations between the Iroquois Confederacy and the United States*, edited by G. Peter Jemison and Anna M. Schein, 66–75. Santa Fe, NM: Clear Light, 2000.

Lyons, Scott. *X-Marks: Native Signatures of Assent*. Minneapolis: University of Minnesota Press, 2010.

Makepeace, Anne, director. *We Still Live Here: Âs Nutayuneân* (film). Lakeville, CT: Co-production of MAKEPEACE LLC and the Independent Television Service (ITVS), 2010.

Mann, Barbara Alice. *Iroquoian Women: The Gantowisas*. New York: Peter Lang, 2004.

Mann, Barbara Alice, and Jerry L. Fields. "A Sign in the Sky: Dating the League of the Haudenosaunee." *American Indian Culture and Research Journal* 21, no. 2 (1997): 105–63.

Martin, Lee-Ann. "Shelley Niro: Flying Woman (Bay of Quinte Mohawk)." In *After the Storm: The Eiteljorg Fellowship for Native American Fine Art, 2001*, edited by W. Jackson Rushing III, 61–73. Indianapolis, IN: Eiteljorg Museum of American Indians and Western Art, 2001.

Martin-Hill, Dawn, director. *Jidwá: doh: Let's Become Again* (documentary film). Brantford, ON: Lock 3 Media, 2005.

———. *Okwànistenhsera: Mothers of Our Nations* (documentary film). Brantford, ON: Lock 3 Media, 2006.

———. *Sewatokwa'tshera't: The Dish with One Spoon* (documentary film). Brantford, ON: Lock 3 Media, 2008.

McClintock, Anne. *Imperial Leather: Race, Gender, and Sexuality in the Colonial Context*. New York: Routledge, 1995.

McIvor, Sharon. "Aboriginal Women Unmasked: Using Equality Litigation to Advance Women's Rights." *Canadian Journal of Women and Law* 16, no. 106 (2004): 106–36.

Medak-Saltzman, Danika. "From Vanishing American to Indigenous Futurisms: Moving Beyond Native Portrayals in Hollywood Horror and Science Fiction." Unpublished manuscript. N.d.

Miller, J. R. *Skyscrapers Hide the Heavens: A History of Indian-White Relations in Canada.* 3rd ed. Buffalo, NY: University of Toronto Press, 2000.

Mitchell, Joseph. "The Mohawks in High Steel." In *Apologies to the Iroquois*, edited by Edmund Wilson, 1–36. New York: Vintage, 1960.

Mohawk, John. "The Canandaigua Treaty in Historical Perspective." In *Treaty of Canandaigua 1794: 200 Years of Treaty Relations between the Iroquois Confederacy and the United States*, edited by G. Peter Jemison and Anna M. Schein, 43–64. Santa Fe, NM: Clear Light, 2000:.

Moses, Sarah. "Onondaga Nation Leaders to Bring Wampum Belt to Washington, D.C." *The Post-Standard*, February 24, 2012. http://mobile.syracuse.com /advsyra/db_/contentdetail.htm?contentguid=u1AwsJp1&full=true#display. Accessed February 27, 2012.

Muller, Kathryn V. "The Two 'Mystery' Belts of Grand River: A Biography of the Two Row Wampum and the Friendship Belt." *American Indian Quarterly* 31, no. 1 (2007): 129–64.

Mutual Life Insurance Company of New York. *The Mutual Life Insurance Company of New York: Accidents, Emergencies, and Illnesses.* New York: 1901.

Native Women's Association of Canada. "Guide to Bill C-31: An Explanation of Amendments to the Indian Act." Akwesasne, ON: Native Women's Association of Canada—Reports, 1986. http://www.nwac.ca/sites/default/files /reports/GuidetoBillC31.pdf.

Newhouse, Seth. *The Constitution of the Confederacy by the Peacemaker.* Revised by Chief Jacob E. Thomas (Teiohonwé:thon). Wilsonville, ON: Sandpiper, 1989.

Newman, Andrew. *On Records: Delaware Indians, Colonists, and the Media of History and Memory.* Lincoln: University of Nebraska Press, 2012.

Niro, Shelley. *Honey Moccasin* (independent film). Brantford, ON: Turtle Night Productions, 1998.

———. *Hunger* (experimental film). Buffalo, NY: University of Buffalo, Sherry Corcoran, 2008.

———. *It Starts with a Whisper* (independent film). Brantford, ON: Bay of Quinte Productions, 1992.

———. *Kissed by Lightning* (feature film). Brantford, ON: Turtle Night Productions, 2009.

———. *Midwinter Dreams* (experimental film). Brantford, ON: Shelley Niro and Jody Hill, 2002.

———. *Overweight with Crooked Teeth* (experimental film). Brantford, ON: Shelley Niro, 1997.

———. *Pensarosa* (experimental film). Brantford, ON: Shelley Niro and Jody Hill, 2001.

———. *Rechargin'* (experimental film). Brantford, ON: Turtle Night Productions, 2007.

———. *Robert's Paintings* (documentary film). Brantford, ON: Turtle Night Productions, 2011.

———. *The Flying Head* (experimental film). Brantford, ON: Shelley Niro, 2008.

———. *The Shirt* (experimental film). Brantford, ON: Shelley Niro, 2003.

———. *Tree* (experimental film). Toronto, ON: Liaison for Independent Filmmakers Toronto and Robert Ariganelo, 2007.

———. *Suite: Indian* (experimental film). Brantford, ON: Shelley Niro, 2005.

Parker, Arthur C. *The Life of General Ely S. Parker: Last Grand Sachem of the Iroquois and General Grant's Military Secretary.* Buffalo, NY: Buffalo Historical Society, 1919.

Pearce, Margaret Wickens, and Renee Pualani Louis. "Mapping Indigenous Depth of Place." *American Indian Culture and Research Journal* 32, no. 3 (2008): 107–26.

Penn-Hilden, Patricia. *Writing from a Red Zone: Critical Perspectives on Race, Politics, and Culture.* Trenton, NJ: Red Sea, 2006.

Pérez, Emma. *The Decolonial Imaginary: Writing Chicanas into History.* Bloomington: Indiana University Press, 1999.

Pertusati, Linda. *In Defense of Mohawk Land: Ethnopolitical Conflict in Native North America.* Albany: State University of New York Press, 1997.

Porter, Tom (Sakokwenión:kwas). *And Grandma Said . . . : Iroquois Teachings as Passed Down through the Oral Tradition.* Transcribed and edited by Lesley Forrester. Bloomington, IN: Xlibris, 2008.

———. *Clanology: Clan System of the Iroquois.* Akwesasne Mohawk Territory, Cornwall, ON: Native North American Travelling College, 1983.

Printup, Bryan, and Neil Patterson Jr. *Tuscarora Nation, NY.* Mount Pleasant, SC: Arcadia, 2007.

Raheja, Michelle. *Reservation Reelism: Redfacing, Visual Sovereignty, and Representations of Native Americans in Film.* Lincoln: University of Nebraska, 2010.

Rice, Brian. *The Rotinonshonni: A Traditional Iroquoian History through the Eyes of Teharonhia:wako and Sawiskera.* Syracuse, NY: Syracuse University Press, 2013.

Rice, Ryan. *Kwah Í:ken Tsi Iroquois (Oh So Iroquois)*. Ottawa, ON: Ottawa Art Gallery, 2008.

Richter, Daniel. "The States, the United States, & the Canandaigua Treaty." In *Treaty of Canandaigua 1794: 200 Years of Treaty Relations between the Iroquois Confederacy and the United States*, edited by G. Peter Jemison and Anna M. Schein, 76–83. Santa Fe, NM: Clear Light, 2000.

Rifkin, Mark. *When Did Indians Become Straight?: Kinship, the History of Sexuality, and Native Sovereignty*. New York: Oxford University Press, 2011.

Rimstead, Roxanne. *Remnants of Nation: On Poverty Narratives by Women*. Buffalo, NY: University of Toronto Press, 2001.

Ryan, Allan J. "I Enjoy Being a Mohawk Girl: The Cool and Comic Character of Shelley Niro's Photography." *American Indian Art Magazine* 20, no. 1 (1994): 44–53.

Seneca Nation of Indians. "Seneca Nation Identifies Major Shortcomings of Competition in Fight for Federal Hydro License." News article posted on website March 7, 2013. http://sni.org/news/2013/03/seneca-nation-identifies-major-shortcomings-of-competition-in-fight-for-federal-hydro-license/.

Sheridan, Joe, and Roronhiaweken Dan Longboat. "The Haudenosaunee Imagination and the Ecology of the Sacred." *Space and Culture* 9, no. 4 (2006): 365–81.

Silko, Leslie Marmon. *The Turquoise Ledge: A Memoir*. New York: Penguin, 2010.

———. "Yellow Woman and a Beauty of the Spirit." *Los Angeles Times Sunday Magazine*, December 29, 1994.

Simpson, Audra. "From White into Red: Captivity Narratives as Alchemies of Race and Citizenship." *American Quarterly* 60, no. 2 (2008): 251–57.

———. "On Ethnographic Refusal: Indigeneity, 'Voice,' and Colonial Citizenship." *Junctures* 9 (2007): 67–80.

———. "Paths toward a Mohawk Nation: Narratives of Citizenship and Nationhood in Kahnawake." In *Political Theory and the Rights of Indigenous Peoples*, edited by Duncan Ivison, Paul Patton, and Will Sanders, 113–36. Cambridge: Cambridge University Press, 2000.

Singer, Beverly. *Wiping the War Paint off the Lens: Native American Film and Video*. Minneapolis: University of Minnesota Press, 2001.

Smith, Andrea. *Conquest: Sexual Violence and American Indian Genocide*. Cambridge, MA: South End, 2005.

Snow, Dean R., Charles T. Gehring, and William A. Starna, eds. *In Mohawk Country: Early Narratives about a Native People*. Syracuse, NY: Syracuse University Press, 1996.

Spahr, Juliana. "The 90s." *boundary 2* 36, no. 3 (2009): 159–82.

Speck, F. G. 1925. *The Penn Wampum Belts*. Leaflet of the Museum of the American Indian, Heye Foundation. New York: De Vinne, 10–13.

Stevens, James Thomas. *(dis)Orient*. Long Beach, CA: Palm, 2005.

———. *A Bridge Dead in the Water*. London: Salt Publishing, 2007.

———. *Bulle/Chimère*. Staten Island, NY: First Intensity, 2006.

———. *Combing the Snakes from His Hair*. East Lansing: Michigan State University Press, 2002.

———. E-mail. November 22, 2010.

———. E-mail. February 13, 2012.

———. *Of Kingdoms & Kangaroos*. Lawrence, KS: First Intensity, 2008.

———. "Poetry and Sexuality: Running Twin Rails." *GLQ: A Journal of Lesbian and Gay Studies* 16, nos. 1–2 (2010): 183–89.

———. *The Mutual Life*. Philadelphia: Plan B, 2006.

———. *Tokinish*. Staten Island, NY: First Intensity, 1994.

Stevens, James Thomas, and Caroline Sinavaiana. *Mohawk/Samoa: Transmigrations*. Oakland, CA: Subpress, 2006.

Sunseri, Lina. *Being Again of One Mind: Oneida Women and the Struggle for Decolonization*. Vancouver: University of British Columbia, 2011.

Teuton, Christopher B. "A Conversation with Eric Gansworth." *Cold Mountain Review* 34, no. 1 (Fall 2005): 31–44.

———. "Embodying Life in Art." *Kenyon Review* (Winter 2010): 218–25. http://poems.com/special_features/prose/essay_teuton.php.

Teuton, Sean Kicummah. *Red Land, Red Power: Grounding Knowledge in the American Indian Novel*. Durham, NC: Duke University Press, 2008.

Toensing, Gale Courey. "Mohawk Man Accused of 'Stealing' Land May Prompt Resolution of Land Claim Lawsuit." *Indian Country Today Media Network*, January 16, 2012. http://indiancountrytodaymedianetwork.com/2012/01/16/mohawk-man-accused-of-stealing-land-may-prompt-resolution-of-land-claim-lawsuit-72362. Accessed February 2, 2012.

Trachtenberg, Alan. *Shades of Hiawatha: Staging Indians, Making Americans, 1880–1930*. New York: Hill and Wang, 2004.

Tuscarora and Friends Gallery. "200 Years of Tuscarora Beadwork." 2013. http://tuscarorabeading.myartsonline.com/?page_id=40. Accessed April 18, 2014.

Valaskakis, Ruth Guthrie. *Indian Country: Essays on Contemporary Native Culture*. Waterloo, ON: Wilfred Laurier University Press, 2005.

Van den Bogaert, Harmen Meyndertsz, Charles Gehring, and William Starna. *A Journey into Mohawk and Oneida Country, 1634–1635: The Journal of Harmen Meyndertsz van den Bogart*. Syracuse, NY: Syracuse University Press, 1991.

Varga, Darrell. "Seeing and Being Seen in Media Culture: Shelley Niro's *Honey Moccasin*." *Cineaction!* 61 (2003).

Venables, Robert. "Some Observations on the Treaty of Canandaigua." In *Treaty of Canandaigua 1794: 200 Years of Treaty Relations between the Iroquois Confederacy and the United States*, edited by G. Peter Jemison and Anna M. Schein, 84–119. Santa Fe, NM: Clear Light, 2000.

———. "The Treaty of Canandaigua (1794): Past and Present." In *Enduring Legacies: Native American Treaties and Contemporary Controversies*, edited by Bruce E. Johansen. Westport, CN: Praeger, 2004.

Wagner, Sally Roesch. *Sisters in Spirit: Haudenosaunee (Iroquois) Influence on Early American Feminists*. Summertown, TN: Native Voices, 2001.

Wallace, Anthony F. C. *Tuscarora: A History*. Albany: State University of New York Press, 2012.

Wallace, Paul. *White Roots of Peace: The Iroquois Book of Life*. Santa Fe, NM: Clear Light, 1986.

Weiser, Conrad. *Journal of the Tour to the Ohio, August 11 to October 2, 1748*. Charleston, SC: Nabu, 2010.

Welburn, Ron. *Roanoke and Wampum: Topics in Native American Heritage and Literatures*. New York: Peter Lang, 2001.

Williams, Paul (Kayenasenh), and Curtis Nelson (Arihote). "Kaswentha." In *Royal Commission on Aboriginal Peoples NOTES*, January 1995. CD-ROM.

Williams, Ted. *Big Medicine from Six Nations*. Syracuse, NY: Syracuse University Press, 2007.

Wolfe, Patrick. "Settler Colonialism and the Elimination of the Native." *Journal of Genocide Research* 8, no. 4, (2006): 387–409.

Wong, Llloyd. "Mohawks in Beehives." *Fuse* 16, no. 1 (1992): 38.

Woodward, Ashbel. *Wampum: A Paper Presented to the Numismatic and Antiquarian Society of Philadelphia*. 2nd ed. Albany, NY: Munsell, 1889.

Zandy, Janet. *Hands: Physical Labor, Class, and Cultural Work*. Piscataway, NJ: Rutgers University Press, 2004.

Index